ON THE MESA

ON THE MESA

TEXT AND PHOTOGRAPHS
BY
JOHN NICHOLS

GIBBS M. SMITH, INC.
PEREGRINE SMITH BOOKS
SALT LAKE CITY

Published by Gibbs M. Smith, Inc.
P.O. Box 667, Layton, Utah 84041

Book design by J. Scott Knudsen

Printed and bound in the United States of America

90 89 88 87 86   5 4 3 2 1

FIRST EDITION

Photographs in this book, as well as on the front and
back jacket, by John Nichols.

Library of Congress Cataloging-in-Publication Data

Nichols, John Treadwell, 1940-
    On the mesa.

    "Peregrine Smith books."
    1. Nature conservation—New Mexico—Taos
County.2. Environmental protection—New Mexico—
Taos County. 3. Mesas—New Mexico—Taos County.
I. Title.
QH76.5.N6N53 1986   333.7'2'0978953   85-26190
ISBN 0-87905-220-1

Grateful acknowledgment is made to Marge Piercy
and Alfred A. Knopf, Inc. to reprint from
Circles on the Water: selected poems of Marge Piercy.
Copyright © 1982. Used by permission.

To all those people, dear to my heart and to my life,
with whom I have shared the mesa.

ON THE MESA

PROLOGUE

B ecause I am a curious soul, I always begin each day with the newspaper. I am intrigued by hijackings, mass murders, town meetings, and the latest scoop on quasars. All such miracles and astounding events structure my reasons for being. I cannot look at any bee or buzzard, lover or lunatic, without incorporating their fascinating stories into my daily rituals. All together they forge both the positive and negative momentum of my being.

I stay sane, I suppose, because there is a constantly adjusting mechanism in me which balances tyranny against poetry, holy aliveness against atrocity, laughter against nuclear annihilation . . . and so my perspective on life is usually positive, creative, adamantly upbeat.

Admittedly, if the redwoods are dying, I have trouble breathing. Yet when Alain Resnais makes a new movie, I rejoice. The Vietnam War, whose weight I bear yet upon my shoulders, still almost kills me. But let somebody bring up Jonas Salk, and his triumph is a glory in which I happily bask.

The equilibrium I maintain between holocaust and haleluiah has long depended on the fact that I travel through life fairly awed by much that surrounds me. Yet occasionally I get running too fast, I grow absorbed with my own importance (or inadequacy). And then, if I panic because the cars are breaking down, or because the money's getting scarce (or because the kids have become teenage monsters overnight), I begin to lose a grasp on that sense of wonder which has always made my daily struggles worthwhile. And if I am not careful, if my self-destructive impulses allow me to get bogged down in the "rat-race," that balance mechanism I depend on suddenly goes awry.

Abruptly, I find myself in quicksand, crying "Stop the world I want to get off." But just like that I have forgotten how to kill the juice that runs this merry-go-round. I'm over-committed to giving talks, signing books, answering letters, writing articles, worrying about the plumbing. I tell people "I'm so tired!"—but somehow there is no moment for repose anymore.

I must jump in the car, go someplace, travel far from home. Hollywood calls. I work on scripts about nuclear war and Haitian refugees, the deadlines are always yesterday. I have to keep up on current events, make speeches, save the world. A dear friend dies, and I cannot stand the loss. I wake up each morning with a sense of urgency: so many things to do, so many people to meet. Frantically, I try to arrange time for puttering in my garden, for fishing in the Rio Grande Gorge, for simply loving the people I love. But it's impossible to relax, I am always behind the eight ball, the producer is growing anxious, my asthma attacks get worse. I have moral commitments, political commitments, business commitments, personal commitments—to children, to publishers, to film studios, to friends, to tax collectors, to the wide earth. Though terrified of flying, I take airplanes, thus minimizing the time lost in my busy schedule. Desperately, I juggle all these "important" things I must accomplish. "Quality" goes out of my experience; mind-numbing quantity takes over. And I start losing interest in the "bigger picture." I have lost the thread, I am "strung out," depressed, discouraged.

Naturally, I also feel guilty for wanting to withdraw, bag it all, be selfish, flee from my obligations. I resent the people around me whom I've encouraged to make demands on my time, my energy, my soul. But most of all I resent myself, the cavalier and stupid being—after all—who has fabricated the frenetic web in which I flounder.

Thus harried, I am afraid of the damage I may be doing to

myself (the typical Type-A personality). Yet my goal of a more tranquil and organized existence recedes farther away as each new dawn rises. Outwardly, I try to seem positive. Inwardly, I mope and grumble, brood and sulk. My brain feels dulled. "Never lose a holy curiosity," Einstein cautioned. But, petulently ignoring him, I lose it.

Soon, however, I am also bored stiff by my own crapehanging. Despair, I believe, is a pretty self-indulgent affectation, the hand-maiden of self-pity, and a feeling to be scorned. Yet there it is, lodged in my bones, big as life.

How, with all the freedom bequeathed me, did I suddenly wind up in such a dither?

Finally, I collapse. Gloom breaks down the ramparts, rushes in, takes over. The pessimistic werewolf inside me sprouts long hair and howls at the moon. And the surrounding world, viewed by my lopsided eyeballs, becomes a grotesque parody of itself. Focusing primarily on negative events, I cannot escape a morbid awareness of the slaughterhouse. The cynic in me grows bold. In fact, almost gleefully I wallow in facts and figures that forecast nothing but doom.

For example, everywhere I turn I learn that the greenhouse effect is on. The North Pole is melting. Warmed by a polluted atmosphere, the eastern half of Antarctica could break off and drop into the briny deep. This would raise oceans by two hundred feet, placing the eastern U.S. shoreline in western Pennsylvania! And scientists proclaim that although the earth has been around for 4.6 billion years, it may take only *fifty* more years to kill it! Finally, it looks like curtains this time. Might as well eat, drink, and be merry, for tomorrow looks impossible. If carbon monoxide don't get us, Dr. Strangelove will turn the trick. And what is the meaning of a single life (*my* life) against the negative odds cast by humanity's vast indifference toward its own survival?

Yet always in the past, at some point in my gloom and doomsaying, a miracle was triggered in me. And just as I began to feel that life's brutal riddles were too difficult for solving, I would realize (once again) what I have always known:

that the only worthwhile struggle on earth is the attempt to solve those riddles.

I have never understood why some mysterious cell has triggered in me a need not to collapse entirely and give up. I only know that I am always eternally grateful for the reprieve. No doubt we owe our survival as a species to those magic impulses in all of us.

"To affirm life is to deepen, to make more inward, and to exalt the will to live," said Albert Schweitzer. And somehow, at the depth of my personal despair, that epigram, and a dozen others like it, worm their way into my head and cannot be ignored.

With that (it never fails!) I have sudden powerful urges to change my negative habits. From out of the sticky darkness hurtle lusts to grow whole again. In almost beatific panic I realize that my role should be to soar with angels, sing praises, be arrogant like Nicaragua. And *heal* my whining self in order to function with hope instead of with all that banal wretchedness.

Accompanying this abrupt seachange is a renewed sense of responsibility. The hour is late, I remind myself; I have been dawdling far too long in negative realms, squandering precious gifts. There is no longer any excuse for such impotent behavior.

"When the Amazonian forests or the world's grasslands have all fallen total prey to the gods of economic development and to the devils of human stupidity," writes botanist Hugh H. Iltis, "no one will care to ask 'Who was responsible?' But in fact, we all will have been guilty! Let us then paraphrase the old Talmudic questions: If not us, who shall speak for the flowers? If not now, when?"

And yes, as I struggle to extricate myself from yet another pessimistic binge, I inevitably grow eager to speak for the flowers.

"But how to defend the flowers," I asked myself recently, "when I have gotten so out of kilter with all this getting and spending and laying waste of power that I find it almost impossible, even, to speak for yours truly?"

4

Obviously, a process needs to occur. First, I must heal myself: only a healthy idealist can shoulder some responsibility for the threatened world. Charity begins at home.

More than once, when mired in a daze and a desperation, I have recalled the words of Thoreau. "Live in each season as it passes," the man wrote. "Breathe the air, drink the drink, taste the fruit, and resign yourself to the influences of each. . . ."

Okay, fair enough. Pulling out my tattered *Walden* I read a few chapters, and am reminded that I grew up in a family of naturalists. Actually, I spent most of my childhood out of doors. Hence, I am familiar with the curative powers of the natural world. In fact, I have already turned to that world more than once in time of need: how silly of me to forget.

And to top it all off, for fifteen years I have lived in a high, northern New Mexico valley (bisected by many small rivers that descend from magnificent tall mountains) which is one of the most beautiful natural places I have ever seen on earth.

It happens, then. Quite suddenly one morning I jump up, tired of nihilistic visions, rarin' to change. And without further procrastination I dress warmly, gather up my camera equipment, jump into my truck, and head westward from this green Taos valley in which I live, aiming for the deserted mesa land lying just beyond the Rio Grande Gorge, a treeless almost uninhabited territory that seems to hover with the neutral rhythm of millenniums, as constant as the sky above . . . and just itching to save my soul.

My aim is simple enough: I want that precious balance back again.

As soon as I park my truck and step upon that sagebrush earth, the quiet land envelops me in a protective cocoon of solitude, and all the hard structures begin to melt inside my tense and tired body.

And as I walk out farther onto the mesa, I realize that already the mending process has begun.

ONE

I sometimes wonder how this spare, bony plateau became so hallowed. It has to do, I suppose, with the lack of clutter. Here, my imagination is free to take off because there are no impeding structures. I crave the wild silence it offers, the lack of contact with civilized artifacts, the aloneness I am bequeathed as I wander across the becalmed sagebrush expanse. And I am awed by the reduction of detail in a way that I could never be awed by the cathedral at Chartres, the Taj Mahal, or an Apple computer.

I approach the mesa deliberately, asking for succor. No more holocaust for awhile; to hell with Hollywood; let the North Pole plead with a different savior for a moment—I'm on vacation.

Parking the truck, I slip on my camera pack, squeeze the tripod under one arm, and start walking. My convoluted shenanigans out there in The World fade away. I smell the August sagebrush. Dry ring muhly "muffins" are everywhere. It has not rained for months, and dirt as soft as powdered silk puffs up a little at each step. The frayed half-moon-shaped musical notes of dead grama grass tremble delicately. The sky is glaring, hot, boring.

But I keep walking, growing almost drowsy from the peace. And after a spell I begin taking note of little holes in the earth that must belong to pocket mice. Warrens of larger tunnels were made by kangaroo rats, creatures built for the drouth—they can go a lifetime without a single taste of water. Of course, most ring muhly circles have long been stripped of

7

their frail grassy lattice by the wind. Now their stalks are gathered, like a precious golden gauze, in the gray branches of dead sage bushes.

The scorching day is malevolent, sullen, aching with heat—but that's okay. No horns are honking, no neon blinks, no gloomy headlines accost my weary eyes. I glance around, eager for a flicker of motion, but all alive things are in hiding, awaiting rain. It's so quiet I can almost hear picked-clean bones sizzling under the relentless rays. In places the baked adobe earth still remains patterned in cracks and swirls caused by the trickling water of long-ago melting snow.

My favorite area of the mesa features a small stock pond near an old sheep corral. The pond has been dry all summer; the sheep corral has been deserted since June. In fact, only in springtime do sheep inhabit this territory. Lambing is done at the corrals, a half-mile south of the stock pond; castration and shearing follow. Driving by at dusk, I've seen an old Airstream trailer at the camp, several men around a cookfire, a battered pickup, and a few hundred animals. It's a dream from a hundred years ago; a gentle and solid valentine from the past.

But by the start of summer they are gone, and the dilapidated corral area is deserted. The fresh smell of sheep dung soon dries out, mixing with the wind and dust. It leaves behind a remote pungency that clings to the weathered fence posts, to the silvery hay atop the corral roofs . . . and nothing else.

Slowly—on a withered August afternoon—I turn, completing a circle, grateful for the emptiness that soothes my agitated soul. Though their majesty always thrills me, the mountains fifteen miles away keep their distance. They never loom overhead, they cast no shadows across this lean space. I am granted all the room in the world for breathing.

Snakes and lizards are submerged, afraid of being broiled. And there are no moths, no cicadas, no butterflies . . . no owls nor eagles afloat. All passion is absent today, and that suits me to a T. This land seems to have folded its arms, closed its eyes, and settled in for eternity.

But nothing remains perfect for long: and even in desert places, iconoclasts abound. In due course, then, I notice a man approaching; his stocky frame quivers through the heat waves. Given such isolation, another human being is as intrusive as Godzilla—and my heart sinks. This bowlegged fellow wears a tan cowboy hat, a white shirt (whose sleeves are rolled up on thick arms), purple double-knit slacks, and western boots. Harsh light glints off a pair of rimless glasses.

Drawing close, he removes the hat and wipes his balding cranium on a shirt sleeve. When he speaks, the accent is good ol' boy and right friendly:

"Helluva day, ain't it? Hot enough to fry the devil."

Grinning, he replaces the sombrero and extends a big paw. "Name's I. J. Haynes. I'm a petroleum landman for the William Castle Drilling Company outta Shreveport, Louisiana. You own any property around here, amigo? If so, I can make you rich."

Oh dear, I think: Just what the doctor ordered—a mastermind of megabucks, a plump little hayseed dervish of Progress American Style . . . and I shudder: Is no place sacred? At first, he seems to have materialized from a mirage. But as I ponder this chunky, amiable character, I notice—way over yonder—a large daffodil-yellow Chrysler cocoon with white wheels undulating in the scorching currents. It looks as out of place on the mesa as I. J. himself.

Before I decide how to answer his question, I. J. Haynes pinches his torn pants near the crotch and cackles, "Looky here, would you? I almost coughed up some prairie oysters on that dang bobwire!"

For some reason, I am almost always polite to my enemies. Though often I would like to cast rude insults, or perhaps blow their brains out—à la Clint Eastwood—with a .357 magnum, I usually bow and scrape and smile, mouthing trite amenities . . . while planning to stab them in the back.

And this fellow raises no exceptions to my rule. So while at heart I am instantly defensive and aggressively alert, outwardly I come on like an amiable chap myself. "Yup, sure is hot." "Yessir, you need to be careful on that bobwire." "Nope, don't think I want to be rich—too much hassle."

"Well," he replies to my latter comment, "money isn't everything, I reckon . . . but it's sure way ahead of whatever's in second place."

With that he guffaws—ho ho ho!—slaps his thigh . . . and on cue I'll bet another hundred species go extinct. And as I back away, courteously waving goodbye—"Well, so long, nice to meet you, take care," (and under my breath, "drop dead,")—all around me I can feel panicked little desert flowers atremble.

TWO

But I. J. Haynes is soon lost in fevered ripples of heat, and I arrive at my favorite haunt, determined—come hell or high water—to work on a cure for this worldly malaise. The United States is poised to invade Nicaragua, and I must send in my Pledge of Resistance tomorrow; but today I'm taking a break from those responsibilities. The earth will survive my absence, no doubt; and my resolve will be a dozen times stronger when I return.

The empty stock pond lies not far from a dirt road that travels north-south alongside a barbwire fence. About half the year this road is an impassable quagmire and I am certainly grateful for that—keeps out the riff-raff, or mugs them if they don't look sharp. If I can't get in myself, I just park on the highway a couple miles north and hike south, cheerful as a lark, squuck-lumping through the mud, cursing it in exaltation—mud, the great equalizer of the Taos Valley: *Long live the mud!*

I must climb the barbwire fence in order to reach the pond. A shallow arroyo leads up to the dam, which is a nondescript ten-foot-high earthen structure rising above the gully. Because I once found a coyote skeleton there, I call the gully Coyote Gulch. It's probably the least impressive Coyote Gulch in America, not to mention the most anonymous—but it's all mine.

Coyote Gulch has steep, three-foot-high banks flanked on either side by sage bushes and rabbit brush. Closer to the dam, the arroyo is almost "cobbled" in black stones. At the dam,

Coyote Gulch turns south, arriving at a small clutter of whitewashed boulders that I have named the White Rock Jumble. The dam is eighty yards long, and runs north and south across the arroyo: it's only a few feet wide along the crest. The eastern side drops sharply down to Coyote Gulch. The western slope descends more gradually into the bowl of the stock pond.

Although it is dry now, old high-water vegetation tells me that when "filled" the pond is almost 50 yards wide at the dam, and the water extends west about a 150 yards, narrowing at The Swales, a languidly sloping area carpeted by shriveled brown grasses. The Swales terminate at the mouth of the Western Gully, where small rocks, sage, and chamisa bushes again take over.

About midway along the pond's south shore, tire tracks arrive at the empty bowl. The road leads south to the sheep corral, and is traveled by the springtime herders fetching water for their flock. They back a tank truck up to the pond, wedge rocks under the rear tires, drop a hose into the water, and suck up a load for their animals. The tire prints, which never entirely vanish, attest to the fact that this hole once held water.

But you could never run a powerboat on it, or water ski, or raise a trout—which makes it useless to most folks, priceless to myself.

The land on the north side of the pond slopes up to an area sparsely vegetated by sagebrush and ring muhly. Among them are clumps of winterfat, one of the most vitamin-rich forage growths on the mesa. Wind, and a lack of moisture, keep everything close to the earth here: there are no trees for miles, another factor in the mesa's favor. People like trees: they cut down the wind, provide shade, produce firewood. Lack of trees means more discomfort, more discomfort means less people, less people means more room for yours truly.

Years of overgrazing have added to the stunted appearance, a look I love because it must be a realtor's nightmare. A book on southwestern grasses tells me that ring muhly is a bad forage plant, and often grows on overused rangeland. According to Frank Gould, who wrote the book: "Ring muhly derives its name from the peculiar growth habit it characteristically develops. As the basal tuft becomes larger with continued growth, the center dies out, leaving a ring several inches to a few feet in diameter."

Well, I'm all for "useless" vegetation. It's right up there with blizzards, gila monsters, and rattlesnakes as a positive factor in my kind of landscape.

Yet even the currently lifeless patterns of muhly are interesting to me, and I take several photographs. From a distance the ground seems covered by numerous concentric meadow muffins. During a wet season, countless fragile muhly culms, with their many dainty blades and spikelets, can create a gauzy web that traps light, holding onto it well beyond the dying of the sun.

When in my healing mode, I can find magic in just about anything with a flick of my aesthetic wand, or the cast of my curious eye. For example: a variety of dry, lace-like growths also populate this area. Among these are skinny rust-colored plants boasting a profusion of frail branches—they rise only a few inches above the sandy soil. A member of the buckwheat family, their crisp remnants are everywhere, often creating a filmy blood-colored slash across the earth. By growing so tightly to the ground, even when long dead the buckwheat is seldom uprooted by wind: instead, thin intricate songs are wheezed melodiously off the complexity of branches. The average person might never hear those songs; but I listen to them constantly.

The rising land south of the Western Gully entrance has more sage, less muhly, and a scattering of lichen-covered rocks. Among these stones is a small, arrogantly-shaped boulder whose beautiful north face is covered with green and yellow lichens. A toad might trip on the rock, but never Gutzon Borglum. No matter, though: if it were bigger, somebody else might notice and show up one day with a wheelbarrow. It's things in nature which don't call attention to themselves that lead a long and happy life.

South of the Lichen Rock, the Western Gully turns right, winding across the mesa in a northwesterly direction. It is never more than a few feet deep, and has no walls to speak of: the ground slopes up gradually on either side. Grasses, flat black rocks, rabbit brush, and sage bushes populate this section of the gully. It's wonderfully innocuous and monotonous, perfectly disguised against the prying eyes of any avaricious soul bent on the commercial exploitation of natural wonders. A quarter-mile northwest of the stock pond, the Western Gully widens, growing even more shallow, more undistinguished, more boring. For about thirty yards the bottom of the gully is tiled with volcanic rocks and slabs of basalt so tightly wedged together that when it rains they hold water indefinitely. At the south end of this currently dry "puddle" are two distinctive round rocks placed side-by-side like small islands. Because of them, in a past wet season I dubbed this stretch of the gully the Twin Rocks Rain Puddle.

The miniature puddle-in-waiting is announced by a curious stone thirty feet south of the Twin Rocks. In certain moody weather the stone resembles a winged skull, such as I have noticed on colonial graveyard monuments. My guess is that since the advent of infinity, I'm the only creature whose imagination (and camera) has discovered that image.

Beyond the Winged Skull Rock and the Twin Rocks Rain Puddle, grasses take over. Currently they are dry growths of blue grama, western wheat, galleta, sand dropseed, cheat and three awn, and even some sticky, foxtail-like haredum grass. Sage and rabbit brush grow taller here beside some Apache plume.

A half-mile west of the stock pond is an object that has remained lodged against one rock or another in the gully for at least three years, a porcelain-coated, blue-and-white beanpot, no doubt discarded decades ago by a careless sheepherder. I keep waiting for flash floods to carry it off, but although the beanpot occasionally disappears for a week or two, it always returns, and always to approximately the same location. Therefore, it is not just another piece of junk, but rather an important talisman of my realm.

The beanpot defines the northwestern frontier of my prosaic infinity in a grain of sand. Beyond it, the gully widens more, the vegetation grows taller; there is a stand of four-wing salt bushes. Behind them is a low earthen dam ruptured long ago by flash floods or drunken shovels. But the mood changes here; obviously, it's the start of a whole other mini-universe, and so I choose to ignore it.

At this juncture, then, I usually do an about-face, heading back along the gully. At the Twin Rocks Puddle I often branch left, taking an overland shortcut to the stock pond. My route travels across a barren muhly plain bisected by a single narrow sheep trail. Barely as wide as my two feet pressed together, the trail was made by hundreds of enchantingly stupid sheep heading from here to there and back again during their springtime sojourn in the area. You'd think they would spread across the wide empty landscape, but when they are moving out in the morning, or to water, or returning home at night, they march single file, without straying—

As I do now, letting the sheep trail return me to the stock pond . . . where I discover atop the dam—oh woe!—two surveyors seated like doom-dark corbies on the just-killed carcass of a stag. They are eating bologna and Cheeze Whiz sandwiches and drinking diet cola. The younger one wears a yellow hardhat, Walkman earphones, and soiled dungarees: the older man's eyes are shadowed by the bill of a John Deere baseball cap. Passively, they monitor my approach—immediately I feel like Spencer Tracy in *Bad Day at Black Rock*. I really don't wish to confront them, but in such an exposed place it would hardly be neighborly to saunter past without speaking.

So, hating my cowardly deference, I cough up a cheerful, "Howdy."

John Deere replies, "Howdy yourself."

I ask, "You with the oil and gas people?"

"Nope," says the younger fellow, lifting one earphone, "electric company."

"Oh, I see." And I don't even falter for half a step. Outwardly, in fact, I'm the essence of manly composure. I nod as if I understand exactly what they are talking about, and nonchalantly keep on moseying around the north edge of the dam and down along Coyote Gulch, heading for my truck parked on the road. I don't look back, don't really need to, I can envision exactly what they are up to:

Flipping me the finger, making faces at my back, sticking out their tongues and slapping their thighs while hooting silently, derisively, and—oh miserable coup de grâce!—no doubt also bending over backwards to throw me a couple of mocking surveyor's moons—

Thoreau never had to deal with the twentieth century!

THREE

For as long as I have frequented mesa stock tanks, I've had a dream. In it, a pond full of water freezes over, creating an ice layer thick enough to support me. Then I haul out my old hockey skates, and, on the coldest full moon night of a pitiless winter, I zoom around that small puddle in a delightful trance of pure aloneness and graceful motion.

Often I picture the scene. It's midnight under a bone bright sky. Lunar brilliance dims or obliterates most stars. A frosty halo girdles the purple horizon. The air is so cold it could be a dangerous vacuum. When I circle the ice I cleave through zero silence.

In my dream, a cruelty to the peaceful moment is uncomfortable (and exhilarating) to imagine. The slightest mishap—a turned ankle, a bump on the head—and I might freeze to death in a minute. If the ice breaks, I'm a goner. Still, I yearn for that midwinter adventure. Even during a drouth I can almost taste the frozen pond—poetic, dangerous, unique. I have never been more exposed, more isolated . . . or more beautiful. Eerie light glances off my skate blades; twinkling chips scatter in my wake. Nobody else has ever been brave enough (or dumb enough) to skate on this stock pond on the Taos Mesa at midnight.

That's it, kit and kaboodle—my dream. I am convinced it will never be realized. When temperatures drop that low, rarely is much water left in any pond. For sixteen years I've hunted that ice and never found it.

But most good dreams persist. And I connect briefly with

this one every time I climb the dam of my favorite pond, and calculate the possibilities for rain.

In mid-August of a drouth year, my skating dream is pretty far-fetched. Images of prospectors dying of thirst in the Mohave Desert or of camels collapsing in the Sahara come more easily to mind as I putter around the empty stock pond, taking photographs of the cracked earthen crust atop the powdery dirt. Thin flakes of dried mud curl up in the sunshine. Streaks of smoke-colored alkali cross some areas of crust. In a few places, the tissue-thin mud chips have been lifted by a breeze, separated from the dirt underneath, and lofted off a ways, where the wafer-thin pellicles look like scattered silver leaves.

As the light changes, growing darker and gradually more luminous, I notice the flattened branches of many dried plants plastered against the outer realm of the dusty pond—relics from springtime moisture. They seem like fragile sea growths whose long, tentacle-like stalks have wilted in perfect symmetry, forming large circular asterisks on the floor of the pond. Branches as skinny as nerves, radiating out from a tiny core, begin to gleam as they pick up the twilight shine.

Without the exquisite light, I would not have spied them. But now, during the brief thickening of dusk, their almost threadlike filaments make intriguing patterns at my feet. And they continue to remind me of the sea, triggering reflections, if you will, on the ocean that covered this territory long ago. They resemble brittle and very graceful starfish, petrifying on the doorstep of their entrance into an eternal season.

When I look up, a glimmer at the bottom of the dry pond catches my eye. I go over to inspect what I think will be an accumulation of white pebbles. Instead, I discover a bed of tiny clamshells, maybe three hundred in all, packed together, edges touching, gathered in that way as they ran out of breathing room, l suppose, when the last puddle of water evaporated back in June.

Astonishment lights up the evening. How did these clams arrive at a stock pond on this arid mesa? Do clam seeds survive dry for a thousand years? Did some bird—a killdeer, a sanderling, or a rail—carry one over from a stream across the valley, or up from the Rio Grande Gorge?

Or am I just gawking at yet another intriguing incarnation of always ubiquitous coyote shit?

Eventually, atop the dam behind my camera on a tripod, I wait for the dark. In all directions my view is unhindered for dozens, occasionally hundreds of miles. Hollywood is a million miles distant, nuclear war unthinkable, Haitian poverty invisible. The earth is at my mercy; my mercy is at the service of the earth.

When I face due east, the mesa stretches uninhabited past the one-mile-distant Rio Grande River Gorge, then continues rolling east to the town of Taos itself, which lies at the foot of the Sangre de Cristo Mountains fifteen miles away. Starting at majestic Picuris Peak in the south, the range runs up past Taos Mountain and bald Vallecitos and Wheeler Peak (New Mexico's tallest at 13,160 feet). On this evening, Taos Mountain is peppered in peach-colored rain freckles. Farther north in the Sangres, past Lobo Peak and Gold Hill, rain—taunting in its proximity—is falling hard against the mountains above Questa, twenty miles north of Taos. At Costilla, a half hour further up the line on the Colorado border, the Latir Peaks are illuminated clearly by angels' staircases of sunlight emanating down from holes in angry clouds.

As my eyes swing westward, I can perceive the jagged summits of Mount Blanca, at Fort Garland, Colorado, eighty miles from my perch. Between me and Mount Blanca are a few smaller, softer peaks. Breast-shaped Ute Mountain is almost misted over. Near the Big Arsenic entrance to the Rio Grande's Wild River Section, Guadalupe Peak (east of the gorge) and jagged Chiflo (just west of it) are boldly lit in sunshine. Closer to me (by ten miles) are Montosa and Pot mountains, low humps—heavily forested with piñons and juniper—which at this time are made vague by purple haze. My most proximate hill in the north is two-peaked Cerro de Taos. It stands only eight miles from the stock pond, and is basking in the drenching gold of summer sunlight.

Three small cones directly west of Cerro I call The Noses. Officially, they are known as Cerro Mojino, Cerro Dormilon, and Huerphano Peak.

Swinging south, not much interrupts the view until I reach my favorite mountain, Tres Orejas, the three-peaked hill in the center of the plateau. Domineering pink clouds rise up behind its unique triple crest. Tres Orejas is richly wooded with piñons, and is inhabited by many deer, porcupines, and coyotes, and at least one pair of eagles, who have nested in its cliffs the past two years.

The mountain is five miles southwest of the stock pond. A few miles beyond it lies the "town" of Carson, barely a dot on anybody's map. Seven dwellings—three of them deserted—and an old stone schoolhouse form the center city of this sleepy burg. Horses outnumber people, ten to one. The road to Ojo Caliente used to be unpaved, but not anymore.

Peering beyond Carson, I can barely distinguish the hazy Jemez ridges around Los Alamos. Then, turning southeast again, I swoop across the Rio Grande Gorge and bump into Picuris Peak once more, twenty-five miles away.

Between all these landmarks and the dam upon which I stand, is open, treeless mesa. The sensation engendered by all that space is one of soaring, and I'm faintly aware of deliberately keeping arms at my sides to avoid floating off.

Two red lights are blinking at the airport across the river, and early Taos lights are twinkling. The only other visible human-made structure I can see is the nearby sheep corral. Yet the corral is so weathered it is barely visible.

Then I hear a faint drone originating in the south. At first I ignore it; probably just a small plane aiming for the Taos airport. But instead of veering across the gorge, the engine noise swings toward me, growing louder, more annoying. Scanning the air, I soon spot an incongruous little helicopter. And for a moment the weird machine seems headed directly toward me, perhaps on a strafing run, and I want to flee this emissary from the outside world. But three hundred yards short it turns north, buzzing up along the eastern edge of the Carson road that brought me here.

Yet my peace of mind has been ruptured once more. And an imagination that so recently fled the Hollywood pale goes tinsel again. No doubt, inside that Jet Ranger sit I. J. Haynes and the two surveyors, first class World Eaters peering down at my desolate land through field glasses, plotting the mesa's mutilation. So without further deliberation, I drop a pocket-sized heat-seeking missile into my portable launcher, cock the deadly machine, plot the wind direction, lift factors, and various azimuths—then pull the trigger. Thoreau tosses me a bit of a "tut-tut," then glances off in a neutral direction. There's a faint *boom!* and a puff of smoke about a mile upwind . . . then immediately we jump cut to the author alone and on foot, toting a pack, rifle in hand, hightailing it up into the Sangre de Cristos, fleeing from the law. He eats raw elk meat, sews rabbit skins into moccasins, and sings with the coyotes at dusk—

One other haunt, not contiguous with the stock pond, is an important part of my territory. I reach it on a dirt track extending east from the sheep corral one mile to the gorge rim, where a rough and tumble trail, called a bajada, descends to the Rio Grande, eight hundred feet below. The trail is frequented by a few foolhardy fishermen and -women undaunted by the rattlesnakes, the slippery boulders, the steep, artery-busting climb out.

Near the trail, a wild rock outcropping overlooks the river. After my stock pond visits, I often stop by that dramatic overlook and have a sandwich and a beer, then teeter blissfully unafraid on the precipice edge, pissing with childlike euphoria into the prehistoric canyon.

But not tonight. A reincarnation of that same helicopter

has made several passes, obviously quartering the mesa with nefarious intent. I feel both exposed and humiliated, and heartily wish it would take a powder.

Instead, the damn fool machine decides to land about sixty yards away. I can't believe it. For years I have wandered the mesa without bumping into another soul—now, all of a sudden, in all my sacred places, I'm meeting double-knit cowboys, electric surveyors, even noisy helicopters. My cure is turning into the same disease I came here to escape.

The engine stays running. A door opens slightly, and a bright object—a hand grenade?—zings out, bouncing a few times across a sandy area.

Then a man drops to earth. He seems to be wearing an official sort of uniform: Army? Navy? Green Berets? Unzipping his fly—shoulders hunched, head ducked—he proceeds to take a luxurious leak. After which he zips up, climbs back in, and off they go—brrrrp!—into the wild blue yonder.

Naturally, like all us wild mesa animals, I'm curious. So I trot over to smell the pee, mark it with my own macho scent, and then run down that mysterious object he discarded.

Which (I should've known) turns out to be not a Hamms, not a Millers, not even a Budweiser, but rather a highly reactionary, long-boycotted-by-Chicanos (and me) Coors beer can.

Defiantly, I haul off and kick it a country mile.

Imagine my surprise, then, when a rather husky female voice behind me has the chutzpah to comment: "That was pretty mature."

I face her, geared to pounce, deflect bullets, run if necessary, be witty and urbane if relevant. The full-bodied woman is tall; she wears a baggy faded-purple sweatshirt, a pleated beige skirt, and old boots. In her late thirties, I'd wager; her hair is turning gray; the eyes are electric blue. Plump cheeks, full lips, a defiant chin, and big rough hands complete the picture. In her fingers, held casually, is a sprig of sage.

"What are *you* doing out here? This place is getting to be like Grand Central Station."

"It's nice to see you on the mesa." She extends a hand,

and what else can I do?—I take it.

"You got out of the helicopter? I didn't see you leave it."

The head tilts left, cocked and dangerous: her eyes narrow, the smile dies. "Do you always jump to stupid conclusions?"

"Well—" I'm getting flustered now. "I mean, not many people know—listen, I'm sorry. My name is—"

"I know. The famous writer. The big time trout fisherman." Humorous scorn drips off her teeth, funny as napalm.

Then abruptly she turns heel and walks away, in the opposite direction from where I'm headed.

And the big time trout fisherman is so startled he can't even pick up a rock and bounce it off her haughty noggin.

FOUR

The sacred book of Guatemala's Quiche-Maya Indians is called the *Popul Vuh*. It begins in the following manner:

> This is the account of how all was in suspense, all calm, in silence, all motionless, still, and the expanse of the sky was empty.
> This is the first account, the first narrative. There was neither man, nor animal, birds, fishes, crabs, trees, stones, caves, ravines, grasses, nor forests: there was only the sky.
> The surface of the earth had not appeared. There was only the calm sea and the great expanse of the sky. There was nothing brought together, nothing which could make a noise, nor anything which might move, or tremble, or could make noise in the sky.
> There was nothing standing; only the calm water, the placid sea, alone and tranquil. Nothing existed. There was only immobility and silence in the darkness, in the night.

This passage often comes to mind when I think of the mesa. I have an eagerness for that suspense, that calm, that silence; for the sensation of a placid sea, the world immobile under a great expanse of sky. Instinctively, on an August evening, I find myself at the origins of a universe. Rain is gathering. No helicopter, surveyors, sarcastic woman, or petroleum landman mar the isolation tonight.

Wordsworth wasn't kidding when he wrote: "How

gracious, how benign, is Solitude." The French writer St. Exupery had a letch for the loneliness of the small airplanes he piloted across African deserts. And he nurtured an understanding of simplicity. "In anything at all," he once wrote, "perfection is finally attained not when there is no longer anything to add, but when there is no longer anything to take away, when a body has been stripped down to its nakedness."

The patient and benign mesa is not exactly naked, but it is as stripped down and as clean a landscape as I know.

And now the twilight air grows so still that it seems not to exist. When I walk, the atmosphere offers no resistance. Made almost dizzy by the seductive passivity, I find myself glancing around for evidence of a single invisible current. I stop, then inhale and hold it. The loudest sounds are cataracts of blood roaring through my veins and arteries, the thump of my heart pumping, and some faint, sticky clicks as I wet my lips.

Such quiet air is almost inconceivable. A world so completely halted seems to be an artificial creation of aesthetics rather than a natural phenomenon. It is environment without qualms, sagebrush etched against itself as if into layers of fossilized stone.

I resume walking, almost on tiptoes. Though it is storming in Tres Piedras, the near mesa is so quiet my footsteps are completely muffled—the atmosphere has no resonance. It seems almost impertinent to contemplate taking a photograph.

Late last spring horned larks quit chirping. Tonight, nothing is flying. Feathered beings, in this becalmed oxygen, cannot soar. I picture them perched on the dead limbs of Tres Orejas cedar derelicts, awaiting currents capable of restoring buoyancy. But birds are used to these moments and wait patiently, fierce eyes aglitter like distant stellar pulsations.

Dry grasses throb with faint, argentine luminescence; a slim crescent moon hangs in a clear mauve patch of sky directly above. Everything idle seems to be growing incredibly animated, almost explosively imbued with energy that will erupt when the slightest breeze bearing a raindrop awakens the world.

At last here comes the almost forgotten song of a horned lark. And another. A tiny bell note, no grander than the faint blurt of a mouse. Yet the note twirls past me like quicksilver, small and friendly, and capable—no doubt—of piercing blizzards with its sleek daffodil brightness and peppy lack of ego.

The birds have returned because they know it will rain.

Melting roses streak the north horizon. Due east, webs of undulating mist reach up off the Sangre de Cristos for heaven. Storms keep colliding all around, getting closer. An ominous nimbus band, two or three miles wide, suddenly slithers without discernable motion across the entire valley, slicing the sky in half.

Light is changing, dying, dissolving—but oh, what passionate death throes! I recall childhood days on evening beaches when phosphorous sparks tumbled in sea foam lapping against the sand. It seems a residue of that same flourescence lingers on the branches, pebbles, and bones around me. Dancing surreal light is achingly intense, and I can smell the rain invisibly swelling around me.

Then the air flares up with a glow transforming this dark moment into such a vivid creation that instinctively I cast about for a band of angels, or at least the shimmering outline of a distant saint.

Naturally, I am curious about the physics of this rare light. "The quantum theory," according to Steven Weinberg, "tells us that light consists of particles of zero mass and zero electrical charge known as photons. Every photon carries a definite amount of energy and momentum depending on the wavelength of the light."

From Guy Murchie I learn that "light has weight and can be measured in tons." He elaborates by informing me that the sun radiates "some hundred thousand tons of light per second."

A peek-a-boo moon navigates through obstructions above Tres Orejas: now I see it, now I don't. Taos is socked in by what must resemble a tropical cloudburst. The only electric lights visable east of the gorge are those two red beacons warning of telephone wires at the airport.

Aha! A few rain drops descend from darkening thunderheads, casually sliding by as slyly as the winks of pretty girls. Lark chirps flick out of the sagebrush gloom like twinkling dimes. The entire landscape is constructed of a liquid shining. Dormant plants, and dust-covered stones are fabricated from molecules of light as tangible as droplets of mist. An hallucinatory intensity amplifies all things. Instinct suggests I move my hands ahead of me and actually paddle through the luminosity.

Slowly, breathing light into my lungs, I part my way. Over Taos, a russet atomic mushroom cloud has formed. Rain is pelting down over there, I can tell by the calm blurs at the underside of the cloud, like pencil lead smudged by a bad eraser.

Darkness is happening, yet I cannot really detect the fusion process. Though enormous changes at high speeds covering great distances occur all around and above me every ten seconds, I can't separate the workings of metamorphosis. Such seamless rapidity reeks of magic. Transformations are happening not with motion, but with emotion.

Ring muhly discs seem almost comical, like regimented oatmeal cookies. Then all at once they become gleaming halos of gold and burnished copper scattered across my path. And I swear, I can *feel* those photons prickling against my skin. When a lone horned lark flutters by it leaves a visible wake, a brief turbulent swirl of light tendrils describing the patterns of its wingbeats.

Moments before the release, the entire plain is alight with a translucent, almost subliminal, foam. Just before sleep my body often flushes with a feverish heat. Likewise, on the mesa, with this final burst of gleaming before the deluge. It's a triumph of nature's imagination, radiance in every sagebrush plant and stalk of grama grass. Polished black rocks emit an ebony glow suggesting that just for now they are lighter than air. You could slip a hawk's feather into burnished basalt contours and tickle their blind iron hearts. They tremble at their sandy moorings, almost able—like insouciant spaceships—to hover inches above the earth, tickled pink by the sudden freedom.

Then the last flare-up of crepuscular alchemy dies away. Rocks settle back to earth without a bump. Only then do I notice the Taos lights twinkling merrily—whatever happened to that belligerent storm cloud? Apparently, it simply rolled up the rug and vanished.

Incredibly, it appears that life will retreat beneath an ordinary darkness. And the tempestuous sky? It's almost empty, nearly drained of dramatic clouds and preposterous light shows. What remains is deep purple, fading in the east to a hue only several inches shy of black.

Impossible! *The storm did not break!* In despair, I realize the drouth will never end, this earth will shrivel up and die.

Vagabond, raunchy coyotes, teased to life by the promise of rain, have no tolerance for the letdown. Their sudden blood-curdling babble at the base of Tres Orejas shatters the quiet. Their outraged howls last but half a minute before curtly dropping back into oblivion.

Deciding to answer with an infuriated lament of my own, I launch a high decible plaint, a no-nonsense plea for inundation that terminates with a heartfelt "Screw you, God!" flung apoplectically at the impersonal universe.

God's answer is immediately forthcoming: the voice is familiar, and derives from an area slightly to my left. "God can't hear you, Mr. Nichols. She's busy defending the Sandinistas in Nicaragua."

"You again!" Holy-moly: I think I'm alone and this miserable witch is practically perched on my shoulder. "How long have you been there?"

"Since long before you came along."

"Impossible. I would have noticed."

She changes the subject: "Waiting for it to rain? Hoping for an immortal photograph?"

"Don't call me 'Mr. Nichols.' Nobody calls me that. People call me 'John.'"

She grins, white teeth flashing: "You want rain? I'll give you some rain."

Raising an arm, she snaps her fingers. And with that—talk about blind luck!—six lightning bolts zig-zag sideways across the placid heavens, and from out of nowhere is launched the purple deluge.

FIVE

It begins falling through curtains of western fire into the arroyo a half mile away. Reflections of the dying sun dance in thick sheets of wetness. Yet left and right of the barrage clear air stretches off to infinity.

We climb the stock pond dam and wait there, dry and comfortable, the mesa witch and I. The overhead sky remains polished and neat. A wayward droplet puffs the dust nearby, a mischievous ricochet from "real life," letting us know it's really all in fun, and not to be taken seriously. Tres Orejas (left of the storm) and Cerro de Taos (north of it) are perfectly defined. But The Noses have been erased by the cloudburst.

Another raindrop strikes my cheek and I gasp . . . yet the cloudburst remains tantalizingly stationary. It should have charged by now, bowling us over, leaving us drenched. Rare it is for weather to keep still on this wide terrain. Usually storms gallivant willy-nilly across the flat expanse.

Though rain falls in tumultuous sheets just a half mile west of us, I feel as if I'm in the protected comfort of my living room, watching the drama on TV. After a minute, I become convinced that I won't get wet. Seated on a rock, I clasp arms around my knees, enjoying the spectacle, breathing in the elixer of the storm from sage-pungent breezes ecstatically chasing back and forth across the empty stock pond like kids in new sneakers. Of course, I avoid looking at the woman; she makes me nervous. I wish she would melt, say "goodbye," and split. Who invited her into my solitude, anyway?

"Who invited you into mine?" she replies matter-of-factly,

causing the hairs on my neck to quiver—how did she know what I was thinking?

A prickly smell of damp dust rises; a faint skunk-like aroma floats off the rabbit brush. They mix with the strong odor of sheep manure and sagebrush. Carried over from the three-eared mountain are redolent veins of scarlet juniper and sticky piñon pitch.

Though rain is pelting down, we are still enfolded in silence. The visible deluge is inaudible. Might as well try to hear the wingbeats of small white moths which have been stirred up by the excitement, and are dancing just above the stock pond dustbowl, no doubt anticipating water.

Tons of that water must be smashing into the Western Gully. For almost half an hour torrents are dumped from overhead, determined, it would seem, to annihilate every creature on earth, forcing life to unfold not with measured gratitude for the dampness, but more in self-defense against drowning.

Yet finally, with an abrupt shudder, the storm exhausts itself. A flick of the wind cleanses the air of every turbulent remnant—*whoosh!* I can see The Noses again, and a casual sprinkle of stars behind them. A silver aura trembles over the far horizon. The new mood is jarring in its blandness.

How disappointing. Only as many raindrops have fallen into the stock pond as there are visible stars in the sky. Not even a fist-sized puddle was created in the hollow. The storm was much too brief. And whatever wasn't sucked up by the thirsty earth will be lost before morning to evaporation.

"Thanks for all that rain." My turn for sarcasm.

"Hold your water, Mr. Nichols. I'm not finished yet."

Peace lays down across the mesa; evidently, the drouth will continue. Still, the horned larks keep singing, as if privy to information I cannot know. And those white moths, teased by the tantalizing odor of rain, continue to crisscross the dry stock pond: perhaps they are captivated by their reflections in a mirage of water I cannot see.

I stand, yawn, stretch. Since nothing more will happen,

it's time for me, anyway, to go home.

The moths have stepped up their activity, frenetically twitching to and fro over an empty stock pond. Their primitive dither makes no sense to me. Obviously, they are excited by an electricity I can't feel.

"Don't go," she advises. "You'll miss the best part."

I hesitate, awaiting the outcome of the moths' odd business. Will they join together in a mid-air frenzy of mass copulation? Or perhaps crash-land in the dust and, wings quivering, deposit eggs in the powdery soil? Maybe, on some inaudible command from infinity, they'll suddenly scatter in all directions—zip!zip!zip!—and I'll never know what caused their boisterous commotion in the first place.

Instead, water (which obviously they—and my pal, the female prestidigitator—knew all along was coming) arrives at the stock pond.

At first, I don't notice the silvery trickles slithering out of the Western Gully and through The Swales into the stock pond depression. Not until the moths are literally going bananas with jubilation do I realize the flood is beginning. By then, a puddle has already swamped the little clamshells.

The artery feeding this puddle expands rapidly, swelling to tree trunk thickness, then wider. It quickly splits into feeder rivulets, which in turn are absorbed immediately by an onrushing river . . . as the only flash flood I have ever witnessed roars into the bowl.

Intent on the moths, I never heard it coming. But now there's a splashing, battering turmoil at our feet. Water rushes out of the Western Gully, uprooting dry grasses in its path, carrying mud and dust and silt in its turbulent eddies, spattering off rocks and sage bushes. Branches and bones clack like castanets, birds' eggs break, pint-sized mammals squeak as they are drowned and smashed to pulps by tumbling boulders. Gallons of swirling frothy foam plunge into the pond, which is expanding explosively; the bubbling violence resembles the action of a washing machine, all things tossed, colliding, somersaulting as the water boils in, filling the pond in no time.

The white moths, whose frenetic dancing preceded the event, are now engulfed by it. Lemming-like they dive-bomb into the waves and are killed instantly. To what purpose I'll never understand. The water suffocates them, tears apart their wings and bodies, eliminates all shreds of their blundering existence.

The pond has a ten-yard, twenty-yard, forty-yard width. Scallops of dirty foam bound around its edges. Water bangs against the dam and rapidly rises toward us. Things struggle in its raging eddies and are sucked under. Small creatures are snuffed by the flood: larks, lizards, rattlesnakes and horned toads, some bats, and whole nests of pink cottontail babies. Pocket mice, sheep moths and their caterpillars, perhaps even a few tarantulas, are all destroyed by the crushing water.

A ram-bam quality attends the birth of the stock pond. In moments water rises more than halfway up the dam until the pond must be seven or eight feet deep at its center. The bigger it grows, the more the surface calms down, although a thick, mucky foam continues to swirl boldly around the shoreline, pushed by energy from the incoming water. Toward the end, no longer jouncing and splashing, the water backs up westward into The Swales, now sixty, then eighty, then a hundred yards away from the dam.

Too soon this oblong puddle of muddy water narrows into the Western Gully almost 150 yards from the dam. And as abruptly as it appeared, the river dissipates: the fierce time of creative destruction is over. Last trickles are sucked into the stock pond, and with that the arroyo is quiet again, devoid of moving water. The entire contents of a cloudburst have been captured in a whimsical mini-lake on the mesa, and the drouth is over.

"I don't believe it."

"It's true, Mr. Nichols."

"I really wish you wouldn't call me 'Mister Nichols.'"

A predatory stillness returns to the area. Because I forgot to check my watch at the start, I have no idea how long it took the puddle to form—maybe five minutes, perhaps an hour. The surface is absolutely quiet; the foam has settled down. Bubbles and floating twigs and grasses are stationary; all blood, all bones have sunk to the murky bottom. No sign of drowned creatures mars the surface—no feathers, no survivors. The mesa is wide awake, alert, steaming.

Suddenly, I realize that a coyote on the south shore is drinking. Next, a great horned owl flaps to earth on the north beach and cocks its head warily. Not until it is done watering does the coyote look up.

And, enveloped in ghostly glitter, the two wild things just stare at each other. Hearing a noise and footsteps, a flutter of material, I shift around sharply, expecting to catch that woman in flight. Instead, the dark mesa is already deserted, quiet, faintly star-defined—she's gone.

And my skin ruffles with goosebumps. What kind of a phantom is that woman, anyway?

Rattling home, I sense the automobile almost a half minute before locating it up ahead, slewed at a helpless angle into the shallow ditch. And long before its features develop from the gloom, I know the garish late-model womb will be bright yellow with white tires: the witch evaporated, and now the devil takes her place. I. J. Haynes is slouched behind the wheel, listening to Tammy Wynette on his radio while smoking a Marlboro, as I circle my Dodge: "Hi, there—need a hand?"

He exposes that full mouth of redneck pearlies. "Does a bear shit in the woods? I hope you got a tow rope."

It happens I do, of course. That, and a shovel, and chains, and a tool box. I never travel on the mesa without them.

"Hey, amigo," the landman drawls cheerfully, once I've got his bloated luxury liner safely out and pointed in a civilized direction again: "I owe you one."

But as I watch his big car nudge cautiously up the rutted road, I think: *I'll bet it's more than one.*

And I begin to feel queasy inside. It's nothing new, of course. I always experience that discomfort before a fight.

Still, the whole process at work here makes me glum. I had really hoped to indulge myself for a spell out on the mesa, disconnected from all the spooky realities of life on earth which harry the susceptible conscience. Instead, it's clear that not even the lonely mesa is an exception to the rule. Trees falling in the Amazon reverberate across this fragile plain: and acid rains gathering in distant climes wait for a wind to blow them inexorably toward my beautiful home. . . .

I. J. Haynes disappears into the quiet darkness: the dust settles down behind him. A mouse rustles, soon to give up the ghost, becoming a scarlet munchkin. A puff of chilly air circles once around a sage bush and slithers off along the scrubby vegetation. A breeze rekindles and just-like-that the mesa is a trifle edgy. Impassive, unblinking rocks, so dull at midday, so animated at dusk, now grow heartless—blood will be spilled.

An owl on a fencepost is silhouetted against stellar spindrift. Coyotes made alert by the rain trot quickly through the sage, all business. There are sounds; cattle band together in a soft gully, reluctant to move until dawn; drugged birds perch immobile in cedar and piñon branches near Tres Orejas. Dry white notes of a bone song frighten all the little creatures brought to life by the moisture; a small rodent squeals, and is quickly eaten. Something shiny out there is restless and serpentine, projecting anxiety.

Hunters and the hunted, whom I cannot see, flicker about excitedly on the newly damp mesa; the killing is instinctive and routine. Nature, awake at last after the drouth, is taking care of business. Yellow grasses shine like the spines of poisoned arrows . . . yet barely a murmur disturbs the evening.

I don't want to start my truck again; in advance I cringe against the violent explosion of that motor. And so I linger a while longer, tasting the fragile mesa, which is always good for me, down to the very last drop.

SIX

The meeting is small, disoriented, inconclusive. We are perhaps twenty-five citizens of wide-ranging political persuasions and vastly differing interests. An out-of-state millionaire, whose big cattle spread is up for sale, fears the price will drop considerably if a mess of 345 kilovolt lines bisect his expansive territory. (No crocodile tears do I shed for him. Yet we all toady up to his huffing and puffing, because he's the only one of us rich enough to actually be heard by the Powers That Be.)

Two Taos realtors and condo brokers are concerned that an auxiliary transmission line may deface land they wish to develop east of the gorge. (Nothing would please *me* more. And I make a note to ask them for their definition of "deface.")

A few Carson residents distrust the electricity, but they would like the dirt road between their town and the Tres Piedras Highway paved, according them year-round access to Taos. (Naturally, I sympathize; but actually I'll do anything to sabotage the paving of that artery.)

Resplendent in purple lizardskin boots, I. J. Haynes is eager to gain more recruits for his cause. Many oldtime mesa landowners still possess their mineral rights, and Haynes is offering to lease them at a dollar an acre per year. In his briefcase are form contracts to facilitate the process. "Already," he explains, "seismic testing has taken place." Apparently, our mesa lies along the kind of geologic fault that has been known to produce abundant natural gas. Test wells are planned; and right now, according to Haynes, things look "damn promising."

(Half the room figures this snakeoil salesman is the Devil Incarnate; the other half wonders if they still own mineral rights on their Mesa properties.)

The Bureau of Land Management and the Forest Service are also present. The BLM leases much grazeable sageland to a few sheep and cattle ranchers on the mesa. The Floresta controls the piñon-juniper country of Cerro de Taos Mountain and Tres Orejas. Both outfits deftly manage the territory under their jurisdiction to at least the partial dissatisfaction of almost everyone in the room.

A majority of mesa residents are relative newcomers to this area. A couple are artists; one is a mechanic who works at a Taos garage; a fourth is a counter-culture lawyer; a fifth is an oddball contractor who earns enough cash with one or two projects a year to finance his subsistence wind- and sun-powered operation. Of course, everybody who lives out there wants to be the last son of a bitch allowed to live out there.

I am a mesa eclectic. Though I write in Taos, I earn my living in New York and in Hollywood. Some years ago, I bought a quarter section of sagebrush near Carson, about eight miles south of the stock pond. The land cost twenty thousand dollars. Perhaps one day I'll build a shack there where I can retreat when Progress American Style becomes overwhelming across the gorge. My current home is but a mile from the Taos plaza. I do understand that my mesa escape plan is a luxury most of the world cannot afford, therefore—speaking objectively—the future of my land is no argument for stopping power lines.

Others here (with whom I tentatively sympathize) are some hardcore Taos gadflies. Included in their ranks are Sierra Club members and Friends of the Earth, who love trees, birds, back-packers, and wilderness, but dislike and distrust my friends the small sheep ranchers and their impoverished allies, the local wood gatherers.

Also in attendance are two officers of the Tres Rios Association. Tres Rios is a group of small farmers and other Taoseños (including myself) who have fought many land and water battles in northern New Mexico. We are a clever mix, capable of most any political alliance in a storm: I once heard us referred to as "a bunch of Communist Republicans."

A few less organization-oriented protesters are concerned with the "quality of life" in Taos. They will support the organic food co-ops, and oppose the spraying of Carberyl on spruce budworms. They'll also join hands with The Committee To Save The Rio Hondo in order to control the polluting of a river feeding small communities below the ever-expanding Taos Ski Valley.

Our meeting proceeds apace. One side demands explanations; the other side avoids dealing with the nitty-gritty. A woman quotes from the powerline environmental impact statement; she is concerned that hundreds of steel lattice towers 112 feet high will seriously disrupt both wildlife and domestic animal grazing habitat on the mesa.

A tall gray man angrily discusses aesthetics: "This will kill the valley's last wide-open area! Tourism, our most important product, will suffer."

One young housewife patiently notes that the Rio Grande Gorge, a mile east of the proposed powerline, has been designated a "Wild River" by the U.S. Congress. She presumes, therefore, that paving the Carson Road, building 345 kV transmission lines, or encouraging gas exploration, must all violate federal laws governing such "wild" areas. Apparently, she never heard of the 1872 mining laws, or of our former Interior Secretary, James Watt.

I. J. Haynes raises the spectre of our poverty. And it's true: despite twenty-five years of tourism boom, we still live in one of America's poorest counties. "Just think what a dozen little ol' gas wells could do for *all* of you good citizens," I. J. crows happily at the end of his ingenuous spiel. "Enough jobs will open up to put you folks higher on the hog than Aspen, Colorado!"

Half the audience claps; the other half boos and hisses.

The Forest Service calmly explains that it tries to bring the most benefit to the widest range of forest users. Translated, this means that forest management practices favor Big Timber, Big Mining, Big Brother.

An old Carsonite asks, "Do the eagles nesting on Tres Orejas count as 'users'?" Another Carsonite, who favors road paving, retorts: "Can those eagles fly my kids to school in December when that road's a damn quagmire?" A third mesa resident fears the powerlines may destroy his radio and TV reception: astonishingly candid, he admits, "I can't live without 'The Dukes of Hazzard,' and 'General Hospital.'"

Passions ebb and flow. The county hasn't funds enough to pave that road unless the Feds spring for a hefty share, or somebody's first cousin's ex-wife's brother pulls a deft embezzlement. Not only does the government favor the powerlines, but it intimates plans are afoot to pave the rough dirt road traveling along the gorge rim from Carson north to the High Bridge on the Tres Piedras highway. Scenic "Wild River" areas on the rim could be "upgraded" with picnic cabanas, garbage receptacles, and toilet facilities. Similar development has already occurred on the Rio Grande Wild River Section at Arsenic Springs, and south of Taos near Pilar.

The government's definition of "Wild River" seems to be: "Any paved wet area accessible to almost everybody."

Quietly, I listen. The Sheep Corral Overlook may bite the dust. They may make accessible to the many what right now is visited by only a hardy few. I have conflicts with the idea. Of course, wild country should be for whoever chooses to use it with respect. Yet when access is made too easy, wildness disappears forever. And I recall the plaint of Aldo Leopold, an early U.S. Forester and a founder of the Wilderness Society:

"Man always kills the thing he loves and so we the pioneers have killed our wildness. Some say we had to. Be that as it may, I am glad I shall never be young without wild country to be in. Of what avail are forty freedoms without a blank spot on the map?"

While the chatter continues, I browse through the impact

statement. At home I have many such documents. I began reading these arcane studies almost as soon as I moved to New Mexico in 1969. Usually I find them to be about as sincere in their efforts to protect both human and environmental well-being as is the health warning on a pack of cigarettes.

They have promoted the costly Indian Camp Dam just south of Taos. They have asked to deplete the small Rio Fernando, used by many irrigators in the Taos Valley. They have wanted to expand the ski valley; they have justified a new tailings pond for the Molybdenum Mine in Questa. They have asked to pump town water directly out of the Rio Pueblo, perhaps killing off all the fish in a river which has been badly degraded by sewage effluent for more than a decade. One plan proposed to kill—with Rotenone—all brown trout in the Rio Chiquito so that rare Rio Grande Cutthroats could be re-established in those waters. Another EIS suggested we build a highway "bypass" directly through the center of our last viable agricultural land.

I have also spent hours pouring over plans to level a piñon forest, reseeding it with grass suitable for grazing. Most recently I plodded through the Floresta's fifty-year plan for the Carson Forest, a document which some environmentalists contend is little more than a blueprint for clear-cutting most of the forest at a serious financial loss.

Many of our large battles commence with an environmental impact statement. What follows is a long and wearying process for any private citizen choosing to lobby for a compromise between unchecked "progress" and both natural and human community balance.

Of course, the bottom line with most development projects is money; cost-benefit ratios are calculated on additional short term jobs and rising land values. Sociological testimony is rarely allowed in official court hearings. "Progress" encourages a competitive climate that weeds out the marginal player. In Taos, this raises serious problems. The county is so poor that a majority of its residents are economically marginal. Development, in our service-oriented, seasonal tourist economy usually means ample profits for a few tycoons at the top, while the rest of the labor force, working at menial jobs for minimum wage, remains trapped in a poverty existence.

Hence the working class in Taos County often equates economic growth and Progress American Style with cultural genocide.

Yet since I have lived here, amazing battles have been fought by the underdogs, and extraordinary victories won. So far the Taos Ski Valley, many condominium projects, river-threatening recreational developments, and even a conservancy district and the Indian Camp Dam, have been halted or contained by concerned rebels willing to organize.

Meanwhile, back at the mesa meeting, all the usual clichés are applied. "Kill wildness, and we kill our soul." "You can't stop progress." "But what will be left for our grandchildren to cherish?" "We need more electricity for future growth."

Then a voice from behind me, at the back of the room, declares, "We need that electricity like we need a hole in the head."

Startled, I hunch around, and there she is—that strange rainmaker from the mesa. Now how did she sneak into our meeting so unobtrusively?

After the session, small groups caucus; Them over there, Us over here. Several times I start for the mystery woman, but I am deflected, buttonholed, delayed. We talk to a reporter from the weekly *Taos News*. Awkwardly, we decide to form an organization called The Committee To Save The Mesa. The lawyer among us will investigate legal avenues of approach. My mesa apparition keeps quiet, circles on the outskirts. A good friend, eighty-six-year-old Andres Martínez, wants to research current problems among the few sheepmen and cattle ranchers still located on the mesa despite government efforts over the past sixty years to push them out.

Obviously, we should meet again soon. By acclamation, a

chairperson is selected. She passes around a yellow legal pad, and we all write down our addresses and phone numbers. A feeling of camaraderie pervades this moment, as David prepares to wing BBs at Goliath. But by then my mesa pal has flown the coop as furtively as she arrived. I scan the legal pad for her name, maybe a phone number; but of those many scrawls, which one belongs to her?

We all shake hands, laugh a bit, and enter the chilly night. A small, gray-haired woman follows me out, touches my arm. "Do you think we've got a snowball's chance?" she asks plaintively. "Everything always seems so darn hopeless."

I reply that of course we have a chance. If we persist, we can accomplish anything. It's a speech I have given often, to many weary soldiers. I pull out all the stops, even quoting to her a poet I admire, a Cuban named Excilia Saldana: "The most powerful weapon people have against a common enemy is optimism."

When my pep talk is over, the woman gives me a genuine smile and an abrazo, saying "Thank you." Then she meanders off into the dark, ready to slaughter giants.

I scan that dark for the mesa woman; I scan it repeatedly in vain.

At home I build a fire in the kitchen stove, open a beer, and plow through the environmental impact statement. A new substation to tap the 345 kV line will be built in Carson, no doubt on a portion of my sagebrush land. It will feature sixty-foot-high towers with microwave dishes and dipole antennas. I picture a sort of mammoth R2-D2, in drag.

Interestingly, the company considered nearly a dozen alternative routes. They discarded one, on the east side of the gorge, because it traveled through populated areas. A corridor west of the open mesa would be less disruptive, but more costly. Judging from a map of the chosen path, I calculate that the transmission lines will cruise directly up the heart of the mesa, and—insult to injury—I would not be surprised one day to discover a tower smack dab in the middle of my favorite stock pond.

The new powerlines are justified because they will help ensure current demand, and provide "back-up electricity" in a crisis. Most importantly, they'll meet a need for "future growth" from Taos to Colorado's San Luis Valley.

My immediate thought is that the project will drive our electric bills out of sight. Only last week I received a little pamphlet in my bill envelope, warning me that rates will rise because of a new $400 million generating plant in Utah. Recently, newspapers have decried projects like the Palo Verde nuclear power plant in Arizona, an operation that has created a supply far exceeding demand, and whose costs must be born by current users.

The mesa power lines—like a bag of 5-10-5 on a tomato patch—are specifically intended to stimulate growth. But naturally, the impact statement pays lip service to "Energy Conservation and Load Management." Our local electric co-op is praised for encouraging its users to "conserve energy" by insulating their all-electric homes, defrosting Frigidaires and freezers regularly, operating snow-making equipment at night, controlling electric hot water heaters (and washers and dryers, dishwashers, microwave ovens, stoves, TVs, waffle irons, etc.), and by leaving their Water Pics off when not in use.

Meantime, the economy (and the electric company) encourage us all to install electric heat, buy every volt-supplied appliance on the block, and purchase one, two, many mercury vapor security lamps.

In my kitchen, a file cabinet next to the refrigerator is filled with newspaper articles organized in manila folders under topics as diverse as: Nuclear Power, Farm Problems, Drugs, The Deficit, Nicaragua, South Africa, Economics, Banking, Marilyn Monroe, Environment, Health, Freedom of the Press, Wayne Gretzky, Genetic Engineering, Trout. Daily, I clip and file the papers, hoping to maintain a macroscopic overview of how my community, my country, and the world function. Like many eco-politicos I feel that all lines of connection on earth eventually join up to form a single vital organism. Hence, I figure the implications of a powerline on the Taos mesa ultimately can shed light on the fate of the world—

Meaning that even the boring and marginal mesa deserves no less attention, respect, or concern than the most lush and productive terrain on earth.

So much for the impact statement tonight. Time out for a sandwich, another beer. I'm tired, my mood is melancholy. I do wish just *once* we wouldn't have to fight so bitterly for every little thing we cherish.

Seated on my portal, peering into the dark, I recall the gray-haired lady outside our meeting, listening to my spiel of hope. And I grin, thinking how often I quote poetry to shore up the flagging spirits of friends and other allies . . . and also myself. One of my favorite writers is Marge Piercy. And I think of her work now:

> Despair is the worst betrayal, the coldest seduction;
> to believe at last that the enemy will prevail.
> Hush, the heart's drum, my life, my breath.
> There is finally a bone in the heart that does not break
> when we remember we are still part of each other,
> the muscle of hope that goes on in the dark
> pumping the blood that feeds us.

Well, it's late, and sleep beckons. But I tarry a moment longer on the portal, a trifle expectant, waiting for something to happen. That intriguing witch from the mesa is on my mind, capriciously appearing and disappearing, mocking me with her "Mr. Nichols," her cracks about big time trout fishermen, her definition of God as a woman defending Nicaragua. It wouldn't surprise me if suddenly my phone rang, and the voice belonged to her; or if all at once I caught a glimpse of that lady's graying tresses afloat in my misty back field. . . .

SEVEN

You pull the string on a folded-up Chinese paper flower and it pops into being, replete with many serene oriental colors—so the mesa sprouts alive just seconds after the rain and hustles full-tilt toward its own brand of muted glory.

Although the sky often reverberates with bombastic folderol, the burgeoning on earth is more subtle and restrained. Yet once I am tuned in to the drama, the diversity and energy of its unfolding life forms takes my breath away.

Grasses rise in delicate profusion. Sagebrush grows bushier, adopting a pastel-blue shine. Dry branches of rabbit brush flush verdant and produce bright yellow flowers. Wild milkweed plants pop up in Coyote Gulch and blossom pinkly; monarch butterflies arrive and lay eggs which spawn caterpillars. Overnight, round ring muhly discs become fluffy halos which soon cover portions of the mesa with a gauze that resembles platters of mist or clumps of soft fur. Lemon-yellow blossoms erupt among prickly pear spines on the stock pond's northwest shore. And a band of greasy green nettles matures along the western slope of the dam.

Everything materializes in a hurry, racing against time. The rainy season began six weeks late; August is half over; a freeze could occur on Labor Day; snow should brighten mountain peaks by mid-September.

Moisture makes the plateau shiny, perfect for photographs. In the early mornings, steam rises off the damp earth. Afternoon mists sweep lazily across the reams of sagebrush. A world, which previously smelled of burnt earth and drying grasses, perks up, unleashing a heady redolence. I stash an extra asthma inhaler in my camera pack.

The soft brown soil emits a deep musky odor. From the sage a sour incense of almost medicinal sharpness arises. The bitter leaves of soaked rabbit brush reek of fox or skunk. Mixed in are funky vulgar fumes of sheep dung. Millions of borrega droppings have been washed into foam-crusted ridges along the sloping ground; air currents are lubricated with hits of ammonia from animal wastes. The aroma blends perfectly with all the tart fermentation of the barren flatlands.

Other spicy odors contribute to the invisible brew. An occasional trickle of vanilla fragrance is wafted over from the warm bark of tall pines on Tres Orejas. Four-wing saltbushes just beyond the Western Gully beanpot exude an unpleasant stink that resembles the spray of tomcats. Horehound mint emits a sweet, faintly stinging bouquet.

After the smells, I most notice colors. Rabbit brush green wakes up; its flowers have a cadium-yellow intensity. Low, mound-shaped snakeweed bushes turn apple green, then amber. Hairy golden aster vibrates with pollen yellow.

The mesa, which only yesterday seemed mired forever in burnt ochres, umbers, and sepia tones, flushes with plush pinks, vague lavenders, creamy yellows, and sensuous purples. Even the ugly, kochia tumbleweeds flash pretty, canary-bright branches. Thorny Russian thistles display a coy verdancy. Western Gully Apache plume bears small white flowers that endure but a moment before turning into russet silky seed tufts. And sunflowers blossom at the northeast corner of the pond; their bright yellow petals are the most vivid growth on the mesa.

As water recedes from the western inlet, lush grasses spring up in the muck. Western wheat, galleta grass, muhly, blue grama, and sand dropseed soon carpet The Swales with many subtle tones of green, beige, and yellow.

Farther up that gully, wild sweetpea twines between blue grama stems, producing pink and white flowers. Amaranth prospers everywhere. On higher ground the haredum grass captures afternoon sunlight in its feathery inflorescence. And even locoweed germinates in a few shadowed nooks and crannies, waiting to play a cruel joke on the undiscriminating grazer.

Naturally, as vegetation grows higher and wider, the birds, animals, and insects of the mesa begin to proliferate.

In hot July I could spend an evening at the stock pond dusthole without hearing a sound. But water touches the insect world with an immediate fecund spell, and a noisy evening ballyhoo ensues as a million crickets launch a contest to see who can first wear out their wings.

Grasshoppers abound. Because I'm alert for rattlesnakes, the small hoppers whose vermillion wings crackle as they launch themselves often give me mini heart attacks. I squat, straining down as if constipated—the old Valsalva maneuver. That stops my fibrillations and gets the old ticker beating normally again.

Hours after the water is impounded, mosquitoes and other bugs are running rampant. I begin to see the splash rings of insects being born. It isn't long before green darning needles zip over the muddy pond, chased by aggressive blue and gray dragonflies. Tiny things grab each other, kick and fuss, chew and dismember, eat, digest, and defecate, and then look around hungrily to see if there's anybody they missed: life, elucidated by unending holocaust; the natural world as total war!

However this bucolic slaughterhouse is perceived, on the mesa the spadefoot toads are the first real gauge of the stock pond's awakening. I've read that these small toads spend most of their lives dormant underground: books suggest that the toads sleep for months, "perhaps years" at a time. I have never seen a mature spadefoot, in daylight, on the mesa.

Yet soon as the stock pond holds water, great hoardes of the nocturnal toadlets appear. For a night or two, these mysterious creatures raise a ruckus, bleating at each other stridently as they hop about in a delirious mating ritual I have never witnessed. Since the toads are programmed to reproduce in shallow rain puddles which often last but a week or two, they waste little time in courtship subtleties. It rains, there's water—a mass orgy takes place. Fertilized eggs are cached in the water. And the adult toads vanish, presumably tunneling (backwards) into oblivion, there to await another propitious deluge one year hence.

Spadefoot eggs hatch immediately, and the results—a Cecil B. DeMille production of tadpoles—transforms itself from aquatic bumblers to air-breathing adults in a similarly vertiginous time period. *The Guinness Book of World Records* doesn't list the Fastest Spadefoot Conversion in History, but in his work *The Desert Year*, Joseph Wood Krutch tells of a tadpole that completed its metamorphosis from water creature to desert toad in eleven days.

Considering that most normal frog tadpoles need from three months to two years to evolve into land-based creatures, the spadefoot dispatch is nothing short of mercurial.

One day the pond is quiet; next day thousands of tadpoles are wiggling in the shallow water, feeding voraciously on algae, on mosquito larvae, and (of course) on each other. If I fell in, no doubt these miniature piranha fish would dismember me in seconds. Great bands of tadpoles bob and thrash against the surface, eating insects and gulping air. So many of them simultaneously nibble the atmosphere, that when I hold still I can hear their mouths making a sound like burbling foam on a big head of beer. Dipping cupped hands anywhere into the shallow pond, I can withdraw dozens of squirming polliwogs.

Soon I notice small "clams" zipping through the murky water. And here, I realize, is the answer to that accumulation of shells I discovered a few weeks ago in the bottom of a dry depression. I snatch a clam from the water and inspect the quivering organism inside, pink and fluttery, crowded with legs, feelers, other protuberances. I wonder aloud: "Is it a beetle, a bug, an arthopod—?" Back in Taos, curiosity sends me to the Harwood Library, where a small guide book informs me that I'm dealing with a "clam shrimp." But I learn nothing about how such an animal could wind up in the stock pond.

Spadefoot toads and clam shrimp are only beginning manifestations of the plateau's reproductive tenacity. Hera moths, more commonly called sheep moths, are another. Minutes after the rain they are abundant. Hundreds of them, using odd lackadaisical wingbeats, lazily skim over the sagebrush, waiting for wind to fling them to earth. Almost every day that I visit the stock pond I find dozens of moths quivering helplessly on the water: tattooed across their plump abdomens is the slogan BORN TO DROWN.

Vegetation flourishes; flowers blossom, die, create seeds; rabbits, mice, and prairie dogs eat like pigs, grow corpulent, and copulate with gusto. This in turn creates a rare food surplus on the mesa. Rattlesnakes, hawks, shrikes, and ravens grow plump on horned toads, pocket mice, and cottontails. Horned larks and sage thrashers gobble grasshoppers, moths, and wolf spiders. Wolf spiders grapple with crickets. Glistening orange wasps cruise through hot sunshine seeking little victims. Long-legged burrowing owls chase after collard lizards, the mesa's largest appendaged reptile. Fleeing on their hind legs, these lizards resemble comical little dinosaurs. Naturally, they reproduce quickly because they're dying in droves.

Nighthawks show up at dusk, smoothly cruising the stock pond, nabbing just-born insects. Small Mexican and large hoary bats also check in at twilight, having journeyed over from the rocky cliffs of the gorge a mile away. Red-tailed hawks, sharp-shinned birds, and little kestrels hunt the mesa more frequently. Vultures circle on the fringe of things, over by Cerro or Tres Orejas, or high above the Rio Grande, hoping for a dead cow, a poisoned coyote, or drowned river rafter. Even meadowlarks stray from greener pastures and perch on cedar fenceposts, unleashing romantic lyrical melodies (of threat, defiance, and lust).

When I head home at night, dozens of black-eared jackrabbits and nervous cottontails race frenetically ahead of the truck, seemingly trapped by my headlights, a perfect illustration of the epithet: "dumb bunnies." If it has rained, the lights are also apt to illuminate kangaroo rats zipping back and forth across the slick road in a nerve-rattling game of rodent roulette. When I brake, they halt; when I start up again they make mad dashes toward the crunching rubber of my Dodge Malthus-Wagon. I yelp, flinch, veer, and more than once have skidded into a ditch trying to avoid the suicidal beasties.

For the most part, however, I have little contact with the mesa's shy creatures. Truth is, I am more familiar with the signs they leave behind than I am with their actual selves.

Always I approach the stock pond cautiously, sneaking up through Coyote Gulch, carefully peering around a corner of the dam. Ducks, phalaropes, or killdeer might be feeding in the water. But most often the pond is deserted. Then I can only try to read the stories in the shoreline muck where all kinds of busy tracks intersect. I also attempt to identify feathers caught against the mud.

Killdeer feathers are distinctive, as are those of a mourning dove. The dramatic tail feather of a large hawk is always exciting (or did it belong to a pheasant?). A big white down feather could have fallen from a large shore bird, perhaps a goose (perhaps an eagle, perhaps a whooping crane). Certain speckled breast feathers I attribute to mallard ducks (or black ducks or pintail). Smaller freckled specimens probably belonged to sandpipers (or sanderlings, or . . .). Nocturnal plumage from a nighthawk is easily identified—or did it fall from an owl? After that I'm usually stymied by the varieties of castoff feathers that regularly wind up near the stock pond.

The feathers are easy compared to most tracks. Large webbed feet, little webbed feet. Three-toed tracks could belong to killdeer, phalaropes, or sandpipers. Does this humungous footprint mean a raven, a hawk, or a gull stopped by? Of the smaller bird prints, a majority must belong to horned larks— their repetitious scribbles are the chatterboxes of the footprint patterns.

Of course, intermingled with the busy ornithological cacophony are the animal tracks. I have rarely seen a deer on the mesa, but their hoof prints show up regularly—the deer seem to move exclusively at night. Fresh coyote tracks are made at the stock pond almost daily. They often enter the water, suggesting coyotes will dine on tadpoles whenever possible.

Mouse tracks squirt between killdeer and coyote signs. Kangaroo rat pawprints join the clutter. Rabbit prints are big and easily identified. Other marks might belong to prairie dogs, gophers, rock squirrels . . . or even skunks.

Inevitably, human footprints join the fray. One pair of workboot impressions, caused by a heavy man, circle the pond counter-clockwise. At The Swales I find a cigarette butt—a Kool Filter King. Nearby are the paper tatters of a Snickers candy bar.

It must be the surveyors again.

Feathers, pawprints, even cigarette butts are some ways I have of vicariously connecting to lives on the mesa. Other signs that reveal activity are the droppings various animals deposit. Aside from being a battlefield, nature is also the world's largest latrine. Sheep manure and deer and rabbit pellets are plentiful; mouse doots lie under most any rock I overturn. An owl casting in Coyote Gulch contains pygmy mouse bones and a skull imbedded in beige fur. Gardenia-sized calcareous leavings of shore birds litter the stock pond mud.

Most interesting, however, is coyote scat. Legendary are the tales of what these mischievous predators will devour. I have seen their leavings loaded with the crushed bodies of ants or a dozen apricot pits. One autumn I found coyote turds solidly composed of piñon nut shells! It would not surprise me to locate droppings made up entirely of monarch butterfly wings captured around the milkweed jungle in Coyote Gulch. And I'm still awaiting the day when I discover a heap of coyote shit composed of, say, a digital watch, a few gold-filled human teeth, and maybe a finely tooled leather belt that once belonged to Joe Don, Billy Bob, Lester, or I. J. H.

Then more human prints show up: on the dam, in the soft mud around the pond. A new somebody in low-heeled boots—not a surveyor—has been visiting my ephemeral Walden Pond. A mood, almost of caution, of reverence, defines the prints, as if they were made by someone alert to landscape . . . or by a dreamer. At first—but only momentarily—I am puzzled: then I know exactly to whom they belong—my friend the escape artist, the sarcastic devil woman.

I follow her tracks around the pond, across The Swales, up into the Western Gully. And locate the woman perched on a stone, thoughtfully contemplating some tiny aspect of life ensconced in the Twin Rocks Rain Puddle. "Mr. Nichols," she comments matter-of-factly. "Why are you always disturbing my solitude?"

EIGHT

Y *our* solitude!" I cry at the woman, outraged by her presumptions. "*I* used to have this place all to myself. Now I can't take a step without bumping into you, or into some dumb klutz in a hard hat, or into I. J. Haynes, or flotillas of noisy helicopters. Where am I supposed to escape to any more?"

"'Escape?' 'Escape' is a bourgeois affectation. How many people on earth, even in their wildest dreams, could conceive of such a luxurious and self-pampering retreat as this?"

Too much, already!—I commence a really fast burn. "Well, if that's the case, what are you doing out here?"

"I'm staring into this puddle at an inch-long vitreous dwidget with a slim tail, quivering feathery legs like celia, a hammer-shaped head, and two black dot eyes."

"And of course you know exactly what it is."

"It's a fairy shrimp."

"And naturally you know exactly how they wind up in a temporary puddle on a dry plain miles from any lake, stream, or ocean."

I have left myself wide open, and she is more than delighted to slip in the knife.

"Actually, I do. Fairy shrimp, and those clam shrimps you may have noticed in the stock pond, are crustaceans who are also called branchiopods. Their appendages are both mouths and gills: they eat and breathe through their feet. Their eggs are stored in a brood chamber whose walls are transformed into a protective capsule called an ephippium. When the

65

shrimp molts, the capsule sinks to the bottom and lies dormant. If the pond evaporates, no sweat—the capsule can withstand drying or freezing. Wind often blows the egg sacs miles in every direction. The suspendedly-animated eggs inside can overwinter (that's hibernate), or survive summer drouths (that's estivate). When it finally rains, they wake up and get on with the show."

She smirks—what a smart ass. And who is this obnoxious woman anyway, and why is she compelled to ruin my equanimity with her hostile presence?

"Does that answer your question, Nr. Nichols?"

I fumpher: "Yes . . . sure . . . I guess so . . . "

"Well, then why don't you sit down, bag that camera, take a load off, relax. I think there's enough mesa here for both of us."

It's either that, or stalk off in a huff. So, awkwardly, I settle myself a few feet away, wrap arms around my knees, and assiduously avoid looking at her. Together, we stare into the Twin Rocks Puddle. At first, I can't see a thing, I'm too confused. But after a while I settle down, and various creations come to life in the shallow pool. Greenish-umber algae—or is it plankton?—coats stones and pebbles on the four-inch-deep bottom; small insects, probably mosquitoes in their larval stage, cling to the underside of the water skin. Their transparency almost hides them, yet sunlight, reflecting through their clear bodies, casts shadowy outlines against the pebbly floor of the pool.

Black, oval-shaped water beetles, pumping hairy flippers, are the witless monsters of this micro-world. When our shadows darken their universe, they scramble for the muck and furiously dig themselves into hiding.

Their existence here, along with that of the clams, the fairy shrimp, and the tadpoles, intrigues me. Even a translucent mosquito larva attached to the water skin seems reason enough to marvel. Seldom do we take our hats off to the small wonders which clutter all natural experience. Certainly the electric company's environmental impact statement makes no mention of these hardy little souls. "Think of it," the woman murmurs. "Life takes so many chances in temporary environments . . . and it has repeatedly taken those chances, in triumph, on this mesa, for millions of years."

Lest she wax too maudlin, a bit of branchiopodal doggerel comes to my mind:

> They hibernate,
> They estivate,
> Their hearts almost don't palpitate;
> They never seem to copulate
> And would not try to masturbate –
> In fact, they simply vegetate.
> Thanks God they don't pontificate
> Upon their stupid micro-fate
> Just because the rains are late.
> Instead, they sleep until some date
> When winter, or the drouths abate,
> And then, without a moment's wait
> They start right in to pullulate!

A breeze ruffles her hair, tantalizing, mischievous—almost erotic. I catch the effect furtively, out the corner of one eye. Seemingly transfixed by some puddlebound micro-drama, the hefty witch ignores me. Nevertheless, I'm beginning to think that we may actually be attracted to each other.

Come late afternoon, we depart the stock pond, heading for the gorge, me in my Dodge truck, the woman in her '66 Chevy pickup. On a BLM allotment, cattle graze among anthills and prairie dog mounds. A half dozen calves are prancing, bucking and chasing each other, raising blythe little dust devils in their wakes.

Prairie dogs bark out warnings as we head east on the road to the overlook. On the last leg of the short journey our trucks inch cautiously over rocks in the roadway. At the overlook we park beside an old campfire site, and walk carefully out to the rim of the gorge. Prickly pear flourishes; its spines could easily penetrate my raggedy sneakers. Sharp-leaved yuccas spur further caution. Broken bottles, beer cans, and a Beanie Weenie tin add a touch of home.

We are seated on the rock overhang, eight hundred feet above water. On the east side of the gorge, sheer cliff walls are made golden by late afternoon sunlight. The western walls and the muddy river are in shadow. Encircling storms fulminate grandly, yet not a drop touches our precarious outpost. North of Picuris Peak a rainbow curves out of the valley and disappears in cumulonimbus darkness. My breath held, I take a picture.

As the shadow line creeps up the eastern cliffs, the lyrical descending whistle of a canyon wren echoes sadly. Far below, two vultures circle the west side of the gorge, their wings brilliantly illuminated by sunlight—the backdrop is in shadow. Perhaps a loving pair, they glide around in perfect circles, working the thermals, never once flapping.

Many violet green swallows and cliff swallows zip gracefully past us, twisting and twittering with dashing abandon, the most happy-go-lucky members of the bird world. Soon, however, the swallows retire. Shadow tops the east wall and shoots ten miles in a single jab straight across the mesa and the town to the mountain foothills. Nighthawks are beeping overhead, but it's difficult to locate them in the graying sky. Bats emerge, and the air no doubt reverberates from the inaudible threadlets of their shrieking sonar, another mystifying survival technology.

"If you stop to think about it," says the woman, "a bat echolocation system is impossible. By sending out as many as two hundred random pulses a second, these nearly blind mammals forge an acoustic picture of the world which enables them to catch on the wing insects as small as gnats and mosquitoes."

"You've been reading nature books."

"*Somebody* has to tell it like it is."

The mesa is dark, the sky is overcast; for two minutes the

sundrenched mountains cut a golden swath up the valley. I try
to imagine this place paved and Winnebago'd—and I wince. It
would be like tigers and mountain lions in the zoo. I could
come out here in a lavender jumpsuit and eat Cracker Jacks
while listening to the Dead Kennedys on my Walkman and
reading the latest Harold Robbins potboiler.

Such a vision is depressing. It *does* seem hopeless
sometimes, as if nothing good ultimately prevails. Gingerly, I
ask the woman: "So how really can we deal with the
Greenhouse Effect, memories of the holocaust, and apprehensions of nuclear war? The savagery in El Salvador, and the
Bhopal, India chemical accident that killed and maimed so
many people? Answer me that."

"Enjoy life," she says gently. "Be steady. Never give up."

Indifferent night falls. Below us the slowly-curving river
shines like wet lead. On either side of it, tiny lights are
blinking—fireflies exist down there at six thousand feet. Both
of us agree—we have never seen a single one at the level of
Taos, or on the mesa. The woman decides, "Air pressure must
trap them forever at the bottom of this narrow canyon."

Now hundreds of the flashing insects drift along the river
banks, calming us down, capturing our imaginations, resurrec-
ting a nostalgia for the summer evenings of childhood days. A
few bugs, like campfire sparks, fall into the dashing river
waters, and are swept off—still glowing—toward the Gulf of
Mexico a thousand miles away.

Though she knows my name, I have no idea what to call
this woman. And we've met so many times by now, that I am
embarrassed to ask her—this kind of social awkwardness has
haunted my life. Still, wanting to know her better, I have a sug-
gestion:

"Maybe we ought to drive out here together some
evening."

She stands, flipping a pebble into the chasm, then smiles
in a way that lights up her plump cheeks and plays the imp
within her eyes.

"Uh, I don't know, Mr. Nichols. I kind of like things as

they are."

And once again she departs my company, and never looks back. Remaining seated, I watch her walk to the old Chevy, fire it up, and clunk off in a cloud of oily blue smoke. No name, no telephone number, no address . . . no nothing.

Her one good red brake light gleams in view for almost fifteen minutes, receding far across the mesa. Then it blinks out, and I am left to ogle the stars on my own.

NINE

Los Cordovas is a small, largely agricultural settlement five miles southwest of Taos. Near the heart of the still-intact old plaza is a community center. Toward it, on a bright Sunday afternoon, I steer my truck, bouncing uncomfortably over the potholed dirt road. Beside me is Dr. Paul Sears, a noted author, professor, and conservationist who must be in his nineties. Between his legs he holds a cane; on his lap rests a dated cross-section of a sagebrush trunk.

In the community center parking lot eight men are waiting. I help Dr. Sears out and shake hands with the men. Most are cattle or sheep ranchers who graze their animals on the mesa. After the amenities, we all enter the building and get down to business.

Andres Martínez chairs the gathering. A former itinerant sheep shearer, Navajoland storekeeper, and Taos dairyman, Andres is now retired, but he keeps his octogenarian's body and nimble brain active in local affairs.

Another octogenarian is Bernabé Chavez, who grew up over in Carson, studied at the old stone schoolhouse, and in his youth tended sheep all around Tres Orejas.

Other weathered participants are in their fifties and sixties. One of them, Pacomio Mondragón runs over seven hundred sheep on the mesa; several times I have visited his spring lambing camps just south of Tres Orejas.

Manuel Martínez keeps his sheep on the mesa east of Tres Orejas and south of the Carson post office in the Petaca Arroyo.

73

Delfino Valerio, a Ranchos de Taos cattleman, has corrals and several stock ponds on the mesa.

These men, and a few others I know less personally, are concerned about their future on the mesa. Most have some reservations about how the Forest Service and the BLM govern their lives west of the gorge. About wild river sections or transmission lines, they know little. What they do understand is that each year it's more difficult for them to eke out a living in that arid country.

Mostly, the talk is in Spanish; I scribble notes, pretending to understand everything (when in reality I only catch about every fifth word). Andres and I will carry their observations back to our organization. No high passions or noisy rantings disrupt the meeting. These patient men keep their anger and frustrations under control. Yet the calm concern in their voices is sad to hear. Everybody remembers a time when things were better. Especially over fifty years ago when the mesa was a vast grassland the old timers love to recall. Their memories are not in default: according to Dr. Sears, his dated sagebrush trunk proves that the plateau was once rich in forage grasses.

"We had thousands of animals living on that grass," one old man says quietly. "Then came the Floresta and the BLM. They said the land was overgrazed; they made us get off. That's when the sagebrush took over, when they started to 'manage' the land."

Another man backs him up. "It's like they do with the forest. I remember when the first planes came and sprayed the trees with insecticide near my ranch. My cows got sick. In one year I lost eleven head. When I opened them up their blood was clotted, like plasma; it was just like glue. But those insecticides didn't do any good. Look at the forest today—from Mora to Santa Fe the trees are dying of budworm. They control the forest so much, they stop all the fires, they eliminate most of the grazing until—heck—they manage the health right out of the forest. Today the forest is so inbred that the trees and all the animals have lost their hardiness. They have become diseased and weak and sickly."

Starting in the twenties, they remember, the government began reducing permit allotments almost yearly, diminishing the herds around Taos. Until recently such policies were vigorously applied in Taos County, and today few animals remain on government land. And the surviving ranchers are afraid the Reagan Congress will jack up the grazing fees, effectively eliminating small operators like themselves from leasing public land.

According to one old timer: "Right now, whether you're rich or poor, whether you're big or small, you pay the same grazing fee. That's discriminatory. Whether the quality of grazing is good or bad, you pay the same. And that hurts people like us, in an area where the grazing is not too good anyway. In the old days, at least grazing fees went up and down according to the quality of pasturage and the price of wool and lambs. But nowadays the fees arbitrarily seem to go higher and higher. They don't want us over there anymore. They just want us to close up shop and go home."

Another problem they discuss involves Floresta policies requiring sheep permitees to move their camps every few days, even in mid-winter when snow covers the ground and little grazing damage can occur.

"Each time I have to move my camp it hurts my animals," says a plump rancher. "They get warm in one place, then have to move and bed down in cold snow. I'm not allowed to build a corral to protect the sheep. I'm trucking in hay, but they have to move anyway. I could plow off snow in each new area, but the Floresta won't let me bring in a tractor. They say they're trying to protect the mesa. But what about protecting *me?* "

By contrast, apparently the government will concede almost anything to the electric company, no matter how destructive to grazing, wildlife, and the mesa. And of course a big timber company may practically level entire forests, and a mine can lop off the tops of mountains (as Molycorp has done in Questa) with hardly a question of raising the government's ire.

"El dinero habla," laughs one old geezer. "Money talks."

Our talk shifts to another subject. While tourist roads along the Wild River are paved and dotted with modern camping areas that include bathrooms, cement barbecue pits, and metal picnic cabanas, roads to mesa lambing camps seem to be deliberately neglected. A recreational vehicle can cruise effortlessly to most any scenic overlook of the Rio Grande Gorge, but the tank trucks of sheep people must navigate along nearly impassible dirt arteries two or three times weekly, bringing water to their animals.

"Or how about this?" a rancher asks. "If the Government is so friendly to the electric company, and to the gas exploration people, why can't it drill at least a few water wells in the lambing areas? Then we wouldn't have to wreck our trucks on those terrible roads."

A senior statesman rises: "Years ago we had a well between Ojo Caliente and Carson. Thirty or forty families survived off that well. I myself hauled water for nine hundred sheep. We didn't have any pumps, we did it all by hand. We broke our backs filling the barrels on the wagons. There would always be seven or eight wagons lined up all day long. Those wells are caved in now. But why can't the government redrill them, and make the water available to the ranchers?"

For two hours the dialogue continues. I watch the faces. Chastisement of the government is meted out with irony and a sense of humour. At heart, most of the men are fatalistic. None carry an illusion that their way of life will survive much beyond themselves. When they die, most likely it will be over.

Several of the men are twice my age: I have known them for fifteen years. I hate to consider a Taos Valley (or my own life) without them. I think they stand for a strong history, a viable culture, and a healthy balance we can ill afford to lose around here (around anywhere).

And if their perceptions of life are reduced to quaint myth and nostalgic memory, this valley may succumb at last to the kind of cynical rootlessness that defines and cripples so much of America.

Meeting over, we saunter outside and mill around under a

cloudless sky. The sun brilliantly bakes the parking lot. We all tarry, leaning against fenders, laughing, liking each other, making small talk. Sunshine permeates right to the bone; within moments we are laved in a golden glow. Glancing around, I notice how much everyone appreciates the warmth, especially our oldest fogies, who keep talking, reluctant to leave, tenaciously hanging on to the moment.

"You know something?" says one of the octogenarians, "I just can't get enough of this damn sunshine. When I die, I wish they could fill up my grave with sunshine."

TEN

I must leave Taos for a few days, fly to Los Angeles, get lost in the airport, stay at the Chateau Marmont, discuss writing a film about the after-effects of a nuclear war. Thirty-four Angelenos are murdered during my seventy-two hour sojourn in their city; Circus Maximus is right down the boulevard. At three A.M. I am awakened from dreams about that mesa woman by a silver-haired prostitute across the street screaming obscenities at every white Mercedes and stretch Cadillac that passes. In the hotel swimming pool, one afternoon, swims a beautiful bare-breasted Latin film starlet. Saturday night on Hollywood Boulevard is a gas, stuck in traffic for hours while low riders and break dancers rule the world.

The work is exhausting, traumatic, worthwhile: our dream is to produce a piece of imagination capable of touching humanity's conscience, thus promoting sanity in an irrational world. I enjoy and admire the hard-working idealists involved in the project, yet the minute work is over I am very grateful to fly out, forget it, be gone. I drive up to Taos from Albuquerque, immediately change into shabby clothes, grab my camera, buy an apple and a soda pop at the El Prado 7-Eleven, and head for the mesa, eager to bask in the serenity.

And I might even bump into my mysterious, derisive pal again—Qué no?

Right from the start, each time I visit it, the stock pond is smaller. The shoreline must recede over six inches a day. Yet the weather is damp, unseasonably warm, punctuated by many short-lived cloudbursts. On gray afternoons mist hovers close to the sage, quiet drizzles pass slowly across the wide land. Roads and terrain dry quickly, however; nothing soaks in.

And the woman is nowhere about.

Almost daily, migrating ducks rest up at the shrinking water hole. Teal and ruddy ducks are the most common visitors. Some mallards stop by, more bufflehead, many goldeneye. Several coots feast on the polliwogs and other aquatic critters striving to reach maturity.

On a sunny day in mid-September I spot two Vs of Canadian geese high in the clear blue sky. Although they pass overhead regularly, they rarely land on the mesa. Still, their cries always catch at my heart.

It would be nice to share that emotion with my evasive friend. Yet now, when I almost want and expect her, she seems to have abandoned the mesa.

It is a dark evening at the stock pond. No moon shines, but the stars are plentiful. The haunting gurgles of sandhill cranes carry down to me from a long distance, from high in the atmosphere. I peer up into the night; it sounds like a hundred birds are secreted between constellations. On quiet days, their calls must be audible across entire states and unending grassland prairies. They approach, travel directly overhead, recede toward southern climes. But not once do I spot a bird, or even a shadow tilting through a star.

How quickly the season dwindles! By mid-September most fat and sassy tadpoles have shed their tails and begun migrating from the water. For a week it's difficult to avoid squashing mini-toads underfoot. Still, the puddle teems with polliwogs, and I suspect they'll be in residence all autumn.

Yet a day arrives when an eerie stillness greets me at the stock pond. Amazingly, the tadpoles are *gone*. Oh, a stray polliwog hungrily probes stubby aquatic plants near shore, but that's all; and three dehydrated tadpole bodies lie in the muck, skins wrinkled and flat, emptied of flesh and fluids. As for the rest of their minions—? Cleared out, disappeared, kaput. A massive exodus onto dry land occurred at night while I was elsewhere. For a special moment the pond must have seemed as crazy as a Tokyo subway emptying out at rush hour; surely moonlight spotlighted all those slippery, coin-sized amphibians as they emerged en mass in toadlet pandemonium.

Perhaps coyotes, having correctly prophesied the windfall, waited on the muddy beach, inhaling delicacies. A pair of savvy burrowing owls might have gorged to the point where they could not fly.

And at dawn a great blue heron probably moved in to mop up, filling its belly with hundreds of juicy stragglers.

Whatever else happened, the spadefoots received their mysterious nod from the universe, bailed out of their aquatic prison, and, with nary a fare-thee-well in my direction, they vanished off the face of the earth.

Soon the pond is only half as large as it began. The weather stays warm, no serious freeze is imminent. I search in vain for the distinctive bootprints of a female visitor. Fewer ducks are attracted to the small safe harbor, but pond size seems less important to certain shorebirds. Apparently, plenty of food remains in the water, and in the shoreline muck. I spend a number of afternoons in my buddha position out in the open, observing the antics of phalaropes and snipes, sandpipers, an occasional willet, many killdeer, and some avocets.

It is the avocets who most tickle my fancy.

They have long skinny legs, graceful necks, small round heads, and long, dark, upturned bills. Their necks and breasts are white, their wings and tails are black and white. Like sandpipers and killdeer, they seem quite tame. When I show up, almost twenty ducks hit the airwaves and never return . . . but the avocets are undisturbed by this great k-fuffle. They stop feeding for a beat, giving me the once-over, then go back to work.

On the south shore I sit quietly, watching the avocets dine. The birds are real no-nonsense eaters. Four abreast in shallow water up to their knees, they march forward together shoulder-to-shoulder, sweeping their bills back and forth, stirring up delectable goodies from the goo and swallowing them down with barely a hitch in their militarily precise advance.

The late afternoon is perfect, warm yet autumnal; the sage smell is just right. High demure clouds are gathering unobtrusively in the west; and the helicopter is on vacation.

My body goes slack as I absorb the subtle evening. In drill formation, the avocets wade counter-clockwise around the pond. As it grows darker, a lone nighthawk shows up and quarters the air over the pond, reducing the life span of many insects to but a fraction of a second. On the far shore, a lone duck stares mesmerized at the water, motionless, catlike. Each time the avocets walk past it—*swish, swish, swish*—the duck ruffles slightly, then settles back into a stupor.

When the avocets are near the inlet trench, I shift my position to the base of the dam, only a few feet from the water. I want to see if on their return the birds will come right up to me.

Puffy cumulous clouds in the west keep swelling and expanding. Feathery cirrus clouds, trailing delicate streamers of ice crystals, evolve through some fey patterns in the north. From my new perch I catch the reflected sunset in still water. It's a game I play often at dusk; the mirrored sky is corny, but so what? I love it. I can't stop taking pictures of the melodrama.

Closer come the avocets, scavenging through the water in time to a genetic metronome. I've been watching them for a couple of hours, and they have not quit for a moment. As the nighthawk slices by, its wingtips almost nick my nose. Two doves watering by the inlet trench are visible only because of their reflected silhouettes at the shore.

The avocets draw so close that I can hear the splashing from their beaks swiping back and forth in the water. Apparently, they'll come right to my feet without even glancing up.

But suddenly, about three yards away, they stop. All four birds stare at me for a second, then one avocet gives an odd yelp, the first noise at the pond in hours. Another stretches its wings in a lazy motion resembling a yawn.

I find I am touched and even made terribly sad by their delicate beauty, by our momentary proximity. I am overwhelmed by an awareness of the human-made threats to the natural world, to wild things. I wish to reassure the avocets that everything will be all right. Yet the proposed powerlines seem already cast across the landscape, intimidating future feathered migrants—

Well, it's a brief lapse. The avocets reverse direction, lower their bills into the water, and recommence feeding, heading away from me now, wading through cottony massive clouds shining in the pond mirror.

The world darkens further as night evolves—seamless, without a hitch, no scars; the nighthawk is revealed only when it tilts, briefly exposing white wing bars. Two small bats enter the scene. The avocets become four little ghosts marching around without a break in their rhythm. The bats make slapdash jerky squiggles against the upside-down sky. All this slaughter of little bugs goes on without a sound that I can hear.

Home, work, and civilization beckon. Slowly I rise, trying not to disturb the serenity. When I leave, I strain for no-noise footsteps. Left behind, the bats, the nighthawk, and the avocets keep on feeding beneath the peaceful clouds, under the scattered stars.

Back at the truck the spell breaks, my heart sinks. A triangular vent window is pushed in, the chrome latch broken—both lock buttons are in the UP position. Inside the cab the glove compartment hangs open, insurance and registration documents and tire warranty papers are scattered across the dash, the seat, the floor. Not until I've stuffed this detritus back in the glove box do I realize that my chains, my shovel, my tow rope, and the toolbox are missing.

Ten minutes later, a mile down the road, I slam on the brakes. Off to the right is a green and yellow real estate FOR SALE sign, no doubt planted in the mesa while I was grooving on the avocets. I'm shocked. I've never seen one out here before.

Swinging down, I circle the truck, kicking all four tires, gearing up for a criminal act. Then, taking a deep breath, I approach the FOR SALE sign, yank it aloft, throw it down, boot it, stomp it, spit on it, unzip my fly and write my name across it, then muss dirt all over the glossy tin while raining down a barrage of obscene and violent epithets.

Following this mature display, I march back to the Dodge, floor the accelerator, and haul ass, still foaming at the mouth.

I might as well return to L.A.!

ELEVEN

W hen next I visit the stock pond, I can't enjoy the serenity. I'm nervous, alert, awaiting some traumatic interruption. It's no fun, and soon I pack up and hike out. On a whim I head south toward Carson; not for ages have I visited that town.

One mile beyond the stock pond I spot another realtor's FOR SALE sign, and halt, digesting information on the second such advertisement I have seen on the mesa in sixteen years.

Eventually, I deal with the sign . . . and then proceed south—but not for long.

This time my brakes engage so fast I almost do a brodie, and come to rest sideways on the shiny dirt track.

"I don't believe it, a goddam *billboard!*"

EAT AT THE
ELECTRIC CAFE
IN CARSON
Breakfast Special $1.99
Wilderness Sandwiches $2.25
Coke   Dr. Pepper   Pepsi
Coming soon: BEER & WINE!

I am truly flabbergasted. And although I notice immediately that quite a variety of high-powered pistol and rifle slugs have already perforated the announcement, its message nevertheless stands out clearly. Plus the sign itself— red, green, and obscene as a plastic Christmas tree—appears to be made of planks hewn from giant redwoods. No doubt it is meant to endure for eternity.

While I'm paralyzed at the scene, a ramshackle Edsel clanks along in a tornado of dust, draws alongside my Dodge, and harrumphs to a standstill—the engine dies. A four point deer is lashed to the hood. A gorgeous black-bearded youth resembling Jesus Christ himself rises out of the driverside window (the door is permanently secured with baling wire), and, seated on the window ledge, he aims a scope-fitted .30-06 at the billboard.

"Watch me put a hole in the middle of the 'o' in Coke," he murmurs. Then—K-blam!—he makes good on the promise, slides back into his jalopy, and tries—unsuccessfully—to crank her up.

"Hey, bro'—gimme a push."

Sure, why not? I inch my truck into his rear bumper, and cautiously nudge the Edsel along. His hand, gesturing out the window, urges me to accelerate. Then other hand gyrations wave me off, so I brake, and his car double jerks as he cuts in the gear. From the Edsel's askew tailpipe erupts a mammoth puff of oily smoke, and he's off and running again.

Myself, I count to a hundred before shifting back into first. Might as well let his dustball dissipate before I proceed south again. And anyway, I need a moment to regroup. Things are starting to get a bit kinky, out here on the mesa.

Though Carson is a blink on the map, the east-west road—Route 96—is paved. The old stone schoolhouse is boarded up. In three private homes actual people reside; one abandoned dwelling remains in pretty good shape. Other homes and ruins are widely scattered in the surrounding area. A mile west of the schoolhouse is a post office providing mail service thrice a week. Heading directly south from the school, a dirt road reaches the northwest corner of my land in exactly half a mile. Marking the spot is a sagging one room, tin-roofed homesteader's shack, built in the twenties. Nearby rundown corrals are infrequently used by sheep ranchers driving their herds across the mesa.

I swing toward the metropolis of Carson prepared to be outraged by the Electric Cafe. Yet a quarter mile before I can even reach it, another billboard blatantly offends my delicate bourgeois sensibilities:

UP AHEAD — GOOD EATS, GOOD JAVA
"You Can't Afford Not To Stop!"

The reverse side of this landscape blighter is downright obstreperous:

HEY BUDDY — WHOA! TURN AROUND!
YOU MISSED IT!

I'm so busy peering backwards at *that* travesty, that I almost clobber a moronic cow blocking the roadway. I swerve sharply, almost flipping over, and the cow doesn't even flinch. But I *do* shiver when I catch my first glaum of the Electric Cafe. Atop a thirty-foot long, double-wide, acid-pink trailer sits yet another shrill placard: BEST EATS THIS SIDE OF HEAVEN!

Beyond is a hastily constructed ranch-style archway entrance to a newly-fenced area: the sign dangling on eyehooks from the center of the wood archway reads: ELEC-TRIC CITY TRAILER PARK.

Stationed in front of the cafe is the deer-toting Edsel (left idling by the owner), a new pickup towing a green animal-laden horse trailer, and a battered Chevy half-ton with a white water tank in the bed. I ease myself into this congested lot, and—my heart in my mouth—I forge inside.

On the corner jukebox Freddy Fender croons a country carol. A scruffy dog of dubious pedigree launches a half-hearted glower my way, then collapses back to sleep. A gum-chewing waitress at an end table is gooning at a Waltons rerun: the TV is snuggled on a wall platform above her head. At another table sits a lean jean-festooned hombre, no doubt a rodeo cowboy, and his blond Stetson'd cowgirl. Slouched alone by a curtained window, and enveloped in smoke from an unfiltered Camel, the Deerslayer—his brows all furrowed—industriously plows through a paperback copy of James Michener's *Hawaii*. Seated at the only other table is a sixty-year-old sheep rancher friend of mine who's busily annihilating a bowl of chili.

At this latter table I slide into place, shaking hands with my friend; we exchange greetings in Spanish.

Before either of us can speak again, however, a large bald man, with twinkling eyes and a cigar stuck between Kirk Douglas teeth spins a chair at our table around backwards and plops down country style, letting a menu drift off his fingertips like the final card in a royal straight flush.

"Welcome to the Electric Cafe!" He grasps (and almost fractures) my hand. "Name's Bill Bones! Congratulations! You come to the right place! Order a bowl of my finest chili like my primo here—" (*whomp!* goes the ham hand on my pal's back) "—and I'll throw in a free cup of joe!"

What am I supposed to do, tell the elfin giant to go screw himself? The chili tastes good, and he's right, the coffee isn't half bad, either. Only the talk, ultimately, sticks in my craw.

Bill Bones is a loquacious provider, and doesn't mind who knows it. Snake oil, hucstered by this silver tongue, would do better than Pet Rocks or Hula Hoops. It may not yet be chiseled in stone, but he figures the Taos Valley's future is right here, on the dusty, lonesome mesa. I. J. Haynes is a personal friend, and even though the seismic findings don't yet add up to a boom, Bill Bones isn't worried.

In fact, "Even if they don't get a drop of gas outta the mesa, I figure I'm still in tall cotton! Hey, I'll make my fortune when they build the power lines and pave the main road and that path along the rim. Profits from that'll give me enough to build a permanent joint and pay for a beer-wine license. Mark my words, two years from now Carson's gonna be a regular little city!"

He's even petitioning the State Legislature for a name

change: from "Carson" to "Electric City," the Hotspot of New Mexico.

The prospect doesn't exactly set the rest of us to jumping for joy. Still, I'm surprised at my rancher friend's equanimity. Turns out he's not all that troubled by the powerlines. "If they condemn your land they gotta pay you for it," he remarks philosophically. "And I wouldn't mind that money. Land's probably worth more condemned than it is on the market."

"Not with a paved road running past it," I suggest unhappily.

"Well, if my land values rise I won't spit in church." He grins slyly.

I can't push it. You sure don't talk aesthetics with an impoverished man who's suffered a hard life on a bitter plain all his days. Especially if you knock down ten times his income by writing screenplays for Hollywood moguls. Bottom line here may well be that the price he gets for his barren land if the area develops may upgrade his house, send a child to college, pay for decent medical care.

No point in letting him off scott free, however. At least the spectre of Gas-Wells-On-The-Mesa bears raising. But here again I strike out. My friend has already signed the I. J. Haynes lease contracts, so for the next ten years he'll make a dollar an acre per annum on his three sections of land for doing nothing more strenuous than picking up the check at the post office.

"Well," I drawl, flipping the ace from my sleeve. "Did you ever think about this? Downstate, where Shell and Exxon are drilling for gas, I read in the paper they're paying landowners nearly sixty dollars an acre a year to lease mineral rights. Nobody has to sign Hayne's form contracts. Heck, if they ever find gas on the mesa, a buck an acre will be highway robbery. If they want to sign, at least people should get a lawyer and negotiate a better agreement."

"What are you, a damn lawyer?" By this time the Deer-slayer has joined the discussion.

"No way. But I think I know a bad deal when I see one."

"You get a lawyer," says the Deerslayer, "and sure, he

negotiates a better deal, like maybe ten dollars an acre. But when it's all over and you're tap dancing in hog heaven, the friggin' lawyer turns around and charges you twenty dollars an acre for his brilliant work!"

My friend the sheep man grins impishly. "You know why sharks don't eat lawyers?" When I bite—"No, why?"—he smirks: "Professional courtesy."

Then he sums it all up for me: "I just signed the contracts, don't want no trouble. Way I figure, it's free money."

"And only a fool," adds the Deerslayer, "would turn down free money."

Bill Bones wraps up the homilies: "Me, I'm an optimist. Somebody tells me the world is going to the dogs, know what I do?—I start a kennel. Hey, you can't stop progress."

Irritated by all the complacency, I challenge the Deerslayer. "Wait a minute—how come you shot at that billboard back there?"

He shrugs. "I dunno. Must be something in me that's generic."

"You mean 'genetic'?"

"Whatever."

Okay, I've had enough. Like Marlon Brando in *One-Eyed Jacks*, I'd love to tip over the table, deck Bill Bones with a lightning quick uppercut, then take a step backwards, hook thumbs into my gunbelt, and snarl, "Get up, you scum-sucking pig."

Instead, I shrug meekly, pay my tab, grin at everyone to prove that despite my contrary opinion, I'm a right friendly guy, and make for the nearest exit.

"Hey stranger," Bill Bones calls after me, "You're forgetting something."

"Oh? What's that?"

"God is on my side."

"No she isn't, Mr. Bones. She's down in Nicaragua, supporting the Sandinistas."

TWELVE

Inexorably, the stock pond evaporates. All that is alive on the mesa hurries to achieve its particular fruition. Though surely miles from home, bumblebees and honeybees visit the sunflower patch. Hera moths flip-flop around for a while, then lay eggs and split before the end of September. Apache plume white petals twirl off on the winds; winterfat stalks grow puffier with seed cotton. Pods form quickly in the Coyote Gulch milkweed plantation: each day that I visit at least two monarch butterflies are present.

Twice, rare hummingbirds jangle-zip across the stock pond. The quarter-ounce birds putter briefly at the sunflower patch, then spiral into the sky, vertiginous jet-propelled freckles swallowed instantly by multitudes of space.

Some minor titillation always awaits me at the other side of the dam. I keep hoping to surprise a coyote—but no such luck. I would like to see a great blue heron reflected in the still water; this too I am denied. And my phantom rain-making friend seems gone forever. Yet the aristocratic busy killdeer are a pleasing alternative, the most common "shorebird" of the Taos Valley. A pair has been nesting late near the stock pond; at times the parents go to great lengths feigning broken wings and other distresses, luring me away from their babies.

But a day comes when I catch the entire killdeer family out in the open; the momma and poppa, and four spindle-legged nidifugous fluff-balls, each about the size of a white tassle at the tip of a Santa Claus cap. These sassy, alert fledglings covered with natal down patter swiftly after one parent. The other adult remains fixed in place, on guard while its mate and four preposterously cute offspring prospect along the water line.

When I declare myself by standing up, the guarding killdeer goes crazy, attacking me from everywhere at once, uttering shrill cries, flapping dementedly . . . while the other killdeer speedily leads their chicks up the dry inlet trench through The Swales and into hiding among the rocks of the Western Gully—

Poof!

Next, I startle a bonafidely weird bird. Preoccupied by civilized problems, I blunder around the side of the dam without thinking, and a large dark thing sporting a long decurved bill arises, scrawking, and flaps slowly around the pond, hunchbacked and scrawny, its extended neck all bony and awkward, looking as angular and gangly as a prehistoric invention:

"Holy mackerel, a pterodactyl!"

Guess again, says my guidebook. What we have here is an ibis.

Well, that's exciting: I never saw one before. And, no doubt, having prematurely sent this one packing, I'll never meet another ibis on the mesa.

More cautiously, on another occasion, I approach the pond, settle down beside the lapping water, focus my binoculars, and remain very quiet. Three delicate, herky-jerky phalaropes are feeding on the choppy water, spinning in circles (to stir up mosquito larvae, no doubt), incessantly spearing tidbits. They stay close together, pirouetting and criss-crossing gracefully between each other, lovely personifications of perpetual energy.

On the opposite shore, five stately killdeer banquet with considerably more deliberation. They often stop and stare at the phalaropes, no doubt wishing they'd temper their dizzying style a bit.

Scanning with the binoculars I locate another bird cater-corner to my hangout, a brown-speckled plump little sand-piper. It scoots along the ooze drilling up a dozen mini-critters with every nervous step. What a carnivore! Through my glasses I watch it round a point and head toward me, working the muck the way I work a trout stream, pecking, drilling, never stopping, always proceeding forward, seldom looking back. From time to time it flits sideways to pluck a choice goody from the foam.

Soon, the ravenous sandpiper fills up my binoculars. It never pauses to clean its bill, or to preen a feather; flies scatter in terror before the onslaught.

Oblivious to me, this voracious character passes by only two feet from my toes. I lower the binoculars . . . and gasp. That fierce eating-machine is maybe five inches long at most . . . although that's probably stretching it. I gawk at its smallness.

Then I hear the buzz of a supersonic airborn approach, and look up just in time to see two teal—their downward-curved wings set prettily—splash into the nearby water. Their arrival causes a minor flurry among the phalaropes . . . but the greedy sandpiper doesn't skip a beat.

The ducks swim to shore and waddle among the killdeer, slurping at mucky things with their dark bills.

Everything around me is involved in an orgy of consumption. I begin getting hungry. But I remain seated, patiently watching all the activity as the day changes, losing light, growing colder.

For an hour I barely move. During that time nobody stops feeding. Suddenly, the western sky becomes a lunatic pink: enormous angry clouds are rimmed in shining yellow, while crisp vermillion spears of light shriek upward, almost hysterically beautiful.

I catch my breath. With an almost audible *pop!* the three phalaropes quit nibbling and just thoughtfully bob on golden ripples.

The killdeer stand motionless on the opposite shore.

And the ducks settle into shadows beside the sunflower patch, as if peace might reign supreme on this earth forever.

Unfortunately, at this juncture all hell breaks loose. The first gunshot kicks me sideways, the next explosion rolls me over, and the third report knocks my face down into the mud. I rebound up into a half-crouch, arms akimbo, and as I shriek "Oh God!" I am aware instantly of birds flapping off the water, some twisting crazily from pellets striking them in mid-air, and three male human beings—blasting away with shotguns at me or over me—are near the south end of the dam. The barrage never stops as I raise a hand, shouting *"Hey, I'm here you assholes!"* But then the ferocity of noise (and my terror) tumbles me over backwards. The tilting sky is full of lopsided ducks rising heavily, or skidding toward me, their panicked quacks tiny amid the gun-thunder, their feathers catapulting in weird puffs all over the crazy place as they die, and I hear myself shriek once more during the fusillade, "NO YOU ASSHOLES!" And then, incredibly, there's an eruption of silence, and I'm on my back, mouth agape, panting, watching birds flip-flop at me, splashing in the water and thumping to earth behind my shoulders, while the lucky ones climb away into the blue.

I roll over on my stomach and face the gunners racing excitedly toward me, three men, guns smoking, including a surveyor from the other week.

"What's the matter!" I stammer-scream, both outraged and terrified. *"Didn't you assholes see me?"*

One man stops on half a dime: "Who you calling 'asshole,' asshole?"

By now I'm on my feet, indignantly sputtering: *"I'm calling you an asshole, you asshole! You assholes could have killed me, didn't you even think of that?"*

"Hey, take it easy." The surveyor steps between us, eager

to calm me down. "We were only shooting at the ducks."

"Ducks!" I'm incredulous. "*Ducks!*" I flap my arms like a crippled imbecile. "*I don't believe you assholes!*"

But then all I can do is fume in inarticulate astonishment while they gather up the corpses. My shocked heart is fibrillating, and I feel dizzy—abruptly, I sit down . . . *kerplunk!*

They ignore me. Just gather up their loot and take a powder. So that two minutes after it all started, there I am, alone, slumped in the mud surrounded by evidence of carnage, beside a little stock pond whose surface waters seem to be covered by the deciduous fallout of a huge feather tree.

THIRTEEN

The first official meeting of The Committee To Save The Mesa is advertised extensively, with a blurb in the *Taos News*, and local radio spots for a week. Nevertheless, no horde of concerned Taoseños descends on the public room of Coronado Center on Armory Street. In fact, less of us than before show up. The mesa is not now, and never has been, top dog on the Taos list of endangered species.

Still, we have heart; and enough anger to fuel a decent protest. The community on the mesa, once composed mainly of a few old ranchers, ancient homesteaders, Ivy League mountain men, and California peace-love-groovy freaks, is suddenly changing. Land values have jumped overnight. Outlaws are cultivating dope in hidden arroyos—two weeks ago there was a shootout which miraculously left nobody injured. One old-timer complains that in half a century he was never robbed . . . until this year, when his home was burglarized twice. A fire at an artist's corrals last week is of suspicious origin.

Bill Bones' Carson carnival has not gone unnoticed. His empty trailer park looms large to the conservationists. But the impending liquor license is what has most traditional folks quaking in their Naconas. Bones' Electric Cafe billboards have pushed much of our rhetoric right to the brink of lawlessness. A woman likens them to defecation in church. A teenager suggests that we form a clandestine committee to deal with them properly. I notice he's flaunting a dog-eared copy of Ed Abbey's novel, *The Monkey Wrench Gang*.

We discuss eco-guerilla tactics in America today. A rosy-cheeked raconteur regales us with hilarious stories of The Fox, a noted midwestern eco-nasty who painted slogans on polluting smokestacks, and dumped buckets of putrid factory effluent on the Persian lambswool carpeting the executive offices of offending corporations.

However, most folks at our meeting are law-abiding citizens; they blanch at talk of extra-legal shenanigans.

Yet their fear and frustration is genuine.

"I want to know what we can *do*," a gray-haired lady mutters angrily. "Isn't there a *legal* way we can stop those powerlines?"

According to our mouthpiece, apparently not a whole lot. Grounds for challenging the environmental impact statement are slim. That the wildness of the "Wild River Section" of the Rio Grande Gorge is on the block is a given; but if the government isn't fazed about the transmission lines, there's little encouragement for a private citizens' revolt.

Our major problem is numbers. Few of us actually live on the mesa, or own land there. We have no constituency, and but a handful of votes—a reason, naturally, that the powerline was planned over there in the first place. To be effective we must organize, increase our membership, capture the imagination (and concern) of valley residents who rarely, if ever, visit Carson. We must convince them that a wild and open mesa is important to both the economic and spiritual well-being of Taos.

Attempting to lighten gloomy situations, I often play the jester. So now I suggest we send a patrol out to Death Valley, filch a bucket of Devil's Hole pupfish, and seed them in a mesa stock pond, then file suit on grounds that the transmission lines may eradicate an endangered species.

My levity garners a few guffaws. It also triggers the ire of my old friend, the mesa witch, who abruptly rises behind me, catching me by surprise yet once again. Her rap is not something I expected from such a sarcastic and mysterious soul. Speaking rapidly but articulately, waving some newspaper clippings to which she occasionally refers, the woman lights into all of us. Her opening statement, fired at yours truly, "Mr. Nichols," is that this is no "laughing matter."

Then bitterly she denounces the "anti-people, anti-environment" priorities of a nation whose self-destructive floundering is reflected in every aspect of our own quaint valley's social, economic, cultural, and political crises. She itemizes all the facts of global suicide, and links them to our own little human and ecological holocaust right here in River City. She has done her homework and knows, for example, that already Taos is one of the five most polluted areas in New Mexico (after three open-pit mining and smeltering operations, and a crowded boulevard in Albuquerque).

Roots of our pollution extend back to early twentieth century timbering, she tells us, when widespread clear-cutting spawned soil erosion that silted our rivers with excess trace metals now poisoning even beautiful trout from our most "pristine" waters.

Beyond that, our town's massive woodburning is highly destructive. The torching of illegal dumps goes on every week. Our badly built dirt roads are used by a dozen times the vehicles they can adequately handle: the congestion and dust is appalling.

Too, she reminds us, "Most of the county's housing is substandard, many people still use outhouses, hundreds of shallow wells are polluted by human garbage and animal wastes. Careless recreational development in the mountains, and inefficient (or nonexistent) sewage facilities in the valley, leave our waters badly corrupted. Carcinogenic dust from molybdenum mine tailings constantly blows across Questa, endangering everybody's health. Breaks in the mine's tailings lines continually threaten the Red River."

Her litany about the negative effects of progress continues. She has lived off and on in Taos for eleven years: during that time great changes have taken place. "The crime rate has zoomed out of sight, I don't know anybody anymore whose house hasn't been robbed. I hardly know a woman who hasn't been accosted or raped. I think I'm the only person in town who doesn't own a gun."

She waves a newspaper article. "Listen to this." It's a report on "Crime in America." Our crime rates "remain astronomical compared with those of other industrialized democracies. Our robbery rate is three times higher than in Canada, six times worse than Germany's—"

And on she gallops, cheeks flushed, barely pausing to breathe as she describes how our impoverished county seems to personify the national blight. Alcoholism is endemic; drunk driving is a serious problem. Our accident rate is three times higher than that of the state, seven times the national average.

"In fact, for such a beautiful area," the woman says, "I've never seen so much unhappiness."

And she continues. "During the eleven years I have lived here, there has been a development boom in Taos, we've got electricity up the gazot, yet the poor in this valley, scrubbing hotel toilets, making motel beds, and washing restaurant dishes for minimum wage or less, are just as poor as ever. No wonder there's so much crime."

The woman is trying to do what I often find myself fumbling to accomplish—i.e., give us a macroscopic understanding (in a nutshell) of the situation into which the powerlines might fit. Along the way, she does not fail to ridicule a Reagan Administration trying to build MX missiles, relax environmental safeguards, and start another Vietnam in Central America while destroying many social programs at home.

I admire her chutzpah, and her ideas. Yet I also realize her brazen techniques are not likely to win over this crowd of gentle souls. In fact, the more strident her tone, the more I see our band of protesters growing restless. They shuffle, cough too loudly, and impatiently raise hands at our chairperson, hoping she'll interrupt, calling on someone else.

The woman's bottom line, of course, is that excess electricity and helter-skelter development are creations of the profit motive and little else. "The projects almost brag about their lack of environmental, social, economic, or cultural planning!"

She urges us to take some kind of action. We can't just sit still and let them roll over us. "Anybody who isn't part of the solution is part of the problem," she insists. And then, blushing, embarrassed by her own ardor, she suddenly sits down.

Silence. The meeting room is uncomfortable. Nobody knows exactly how to react. Ultimately, a rather large, lumpy man stands up, nervously twisting his hat in his hands while he speaks.

"We're not Communists here. We don't hate this country. We're just a group of decent, law-abiding Americans trying to solve a little problem using the proper channels."

Naturally, I am compelled to defend the woman. I indicate my support for her world view while trying to pour oil on troubled waters. "Nobody's asking us to be Communists," I say. "And I'm sure this woman is concerned, like all of us, not because she hates America, but because she loves it dearly and wants the good energy of our country to prevail, in Taos . . . and around the world."

Cornball, granted; but the nail-biter loosens up. And I notice that the woman is properly grateful for my support. The rest of us make a list of what we can do. For example, write our congresspeople, write our state representatives. We'll also badger the BLM, the Floresta, and the electric company.

We'll circulate a petition to "Stop the Powerlines," and draw up another to "Save the Wild River." A fund raiser wouldn't hurt; and at it I'll give a talk and a slide show, using my photographs from the mesa.

By the end of the meeting we all feel energetic, full of purpose—we have a plan. A humble one, yes, but a plan nonetheless.

As we disperse, my radical friend approaches me, a different light on her features, one that almost suggests gratitude. "Thank you," she says, a trifle humble at last.

"Always happy to defend another crypto commie pro-abortion atheistic conspirator," I reply with a twinkle. And finally muster the courage to blurt, "Look, I don't even know your name."

"Cassandra," she allows with a grin.

"You're kidding, of course."

"Okay," she fires back instantly. "Maybe you'd like it better as Mary Lou or Billie Jo?"

"I didn't say that. I only—"

"Then why not just ditch it about my name?"

Clearly, it's time to change the subject—*fast*.

"Well, how come I never see you anymore out on the mesa?"

"I teach all day, I take Spanish lessons at night."

"Fine. Then how about a cup of coffee right this minute?"

"Now you're pushing it, Mr. Nichols. I have to go home and take care of Robert."

"Robert?"

"My child."

"Oh . . . you've got a kid?"

"Name me a thirty-five-year-old woman who doesn't."

"Dolly Parton."

"Very funny—goodbye."

And once again she leaves me in the lurch. Only this time I think I've got my foot in the door. After all, how long can two kindred souls afford to ignore each other?

FOURTEEN

E ach day, now, the late summer dies swiftly. Already
grasses, green for but a few weeks, are going to seed, drying out. Milkweed pods split open, displaying white silky
fibers. Ladybugs blown against my jacket cling perilously for
warmth.

Yet the air stays warm, the ground remains soft. At the
entrance to the Western Gully, gossamer strands of spiderweb
material stretched between sage and chamisa branches vibrate
in the afternoon sunlight . . . I circumvent them, reluctant to
cause destruction.

Large robber flies alight on the sand in front of me, no
doubt momentarily weary from searching for smaller insects to
drain in Dracula fashion. On the stock pond mud, even the
miniscule round water mites capture my attention. Though
they are barely larger than the period at the bottom of an
exclamation point, the shocking, passion-pink of their bodies
stands out like Day-Glo bubblegum.

A mouse the size of a rabbit foot darts away from my feet
to poor cover in a snakeweed bush, and freezes. Down on
hands and knees, I peer at it—a silky pocket mouse, no bigger
than half my thumb, one of those creatures exquisite in its
smallness . . . and scared to death. The entire body thunders
from its heartbeat. I'm sure the quaking animal's skin has been
stretched taut over a single organ, a huge (by pocket mouse
standards) heart. The diminutive creature seems almost on the
verge of bursting, so rapid and violent are the palpitations
shaking its entire body. I would like to cup it in my palm, but

like a shot it scoots off, then suddenly pops sideways into a finger-sized hole, escaping underground.

All at once, without warning, a rock in the Western Gully blossoms. Then all rocks in the gully light up, as if from deep within themselves. I have walked past these stones time and again, and they were simply dark, nondescript shapes. Now they have personality. "Hey, Cassandra," I realize with a start, "they are going to be revealed!"

Later, over cappuccino in the Cafe Tazza, I tell her all about it. To begin with, the rocks really aren't black at all. They have an iridescence as variegated as that of magpie feathers. After a moment, I'm not even sure they are dark. A minute ago a half-buried boulder was the color of anthracite; now it seems almost white. Yet the color changes rapidly. First turquoise, then steely blue. Next to it, a rock is permeated with glittering green swirls.

But I can't really get a fix. Black, green, blue, white—it's impossible to pin down such elusive color. Alive with gradations of pigment, their hues fluctuate brazenly—these "dead" things are alive, colorful and moody. A russet patch flares up, gold reigns for a beat and dies. The hard skins are rippling, rising and falling as they breathe. Of course, there is frantic motion in all things we consider inert; electrons spin at cosmic speeds in igneous rocks as well as in air and water. Atoms collide, radiation waves click through the atmosphere: stones have a heartbeat just like you and me.

When I place my hand on the nearest rock, heat seeps into my palm. When I press an ear against the stone I can hear nothing but the echo of my body tossed back at me.

Coy and pretty from this angle, they turn blunt and dangerous when I tilt my head, imperious and cold when I squint, malleable as breasts when I lean closer. Shutting my eyes, I just feel their presence around me, like living fossils, finning lethargically in the dust, proud of their beautiful ugliness, their coelacanthic memories stretching back to the original explosion of the universe.

Silvery green, lead-colored, graphite shiny—buffed by weather, flaunting highlights—there really is a hint of resurrection in the air . . . until I change the angle again reducing them to dullness.

And I sit there, a trifle stunned to have cavorted through so many emotions involving the most stoic portions of my favorite landscape.

"Thanks for the description, professor." She reaches out, patting my hand.

"Don't mock me, woman. I have a delicate ego."

"About as delicate as those stupid boulders, I'll wager."

Ignore her, I decide: after all, we seem to be drawing closer.

And there's a new presence in the stock pond, a hunter of formidible talents. When first I see it surface-feeding, I think: here's a large laggard tadpole. Then I wonder if it could be a fish—some sort of local chub or bocinete. But that's absurd. Finally, I catch a better glimpse of the miniature Loch Ness monster, and realize it's a juajolote (or the newt stage of a tiger salamander), a popular neotonic carnivore in the Taos area.

Years ago, my kids and I captured juajolotes in forest ponds, lugging them home to spend a week or so in dining-table aquariums, where the voracious salamanders consumed pounds of grasshoppers daily, and aggressively nailed our fingers if we poked too close.

Apparently, some juajolotes remain axolotls forever; others head for dry land after a two year aquatic apprenticeship. It is said these largest of all land-dwelling salamanders, who grow up to a foot in length, will eat frogs, other salamanders, even small mice if given the opportunity. They are definitely the alligators of small puddles.

This juajolote adds a sinister touch to the stock pond. One Saturday, Cassandra and I watch it feeding. The phalaropes steer clear of its territory. No other salamanders appear, and

ON THE MESA

how this one materialized remains a mystery. I guess it simply obeyed the main law of arid places: just let a little rain fall and anything is possible.

The mesa is so sparsely populated that any bird, any salamander, any insect, framed by the isolation, stands out with special clarity. The uncluttered arena grants every living thing its unique existence.

Including me.

And never so strongly as on that day when I climb over the dam and spot a dozen big yellow swallowtail butterflies clustered near the pond shore, feeding on, or drinking from (or laying eggs in?) the muck. Their wide wings tremble. I sit still, awaiting a punchline. But nothing much happens. The butterflies continue to quiver and suck at the mud. I clasp my knees, feeling lazy, very peaceful. The yellow-and-black insects change position slowly, wings spread out flatly, resembling gaudy little B-52 bombers cautiously maneuvering around an airfield tarmac.

Then a flock of twenty horned larks sprinkles like seeds onto ground near the butterflies. In quick spurts they trip toward the water to drink. Two larks decide to tiptoe through the swallowtails. But when a butterfly nervously raises its big wings, one lark jumps, triggering an exodus of swallowtails. And when they bluster aloft, whisking off in different directions, the bright commotion also spooks the larks, who scoot away *en mass* and are immediately absorbed by wonderful immensity.

Moments later, while I'm just dawdling on the dam, a rattletrap pickup wheezes to a stop on the Carson Road, and two people tumble out.

Faintly, I hear them catcalling to each other. They act funny, off balance, not at all like hunters. I watch as they climb the fence and head straight toward me through the sagebrush.

No mistake about it, I am their destination. Immediately, my heart sinks: here comes another confrontation. The intruders are drunk, and babbling. Every now and then I catch an obscenity. One has a leather wineskin, and, as they stumble along the edge of Coyote Gulch, he raises it and sloppily drinks.

My first thought is to flee up the Western Gully. But for miles I really have no place to hide. Suppose they've got a gun? I don't want to enflame their . . . suspicion? ire? their hunting instinct? . . . by running. Straining my eyes, I try to see if they carry weapons. All it takes is a little pistol, I think: one tiny lead ball. They are drunk. Perhaps they own this land and consider me a trespasser. Fears of the racial tension traumatizing our valley rise in me. Maybe they want no gringo taking pictures of their mesa. Maybe they think *I'm* a hunter, or a surveyor, or (God forbid!) a real estate agent—

As they draw closer I realize they're just teenagers— seventeen or eighteen years old. They don't wave . . . I make no greeting either. If I put away my camera I can use the tripod for a weapon. But if they don't intend to harm me, the gesture might seem provocative. Better to remain calm, a photographer on a dam, enthralled by the mesa's beauty.

In a bee-line for me they stumble closer; it develops like a spooky High Noon confrontation. They curse, making surly exclamations as they skid on the slick mud. And keep on coming with no-nonsense, boozed-up determination.

Scrabbling up the southern slope of the dam they plow toward me, unsmiling, unfriendly, unrelenting. Timidly, I raise a hand, grin, and nod casually: "How you doin'?" No response. They eye me with curious coldness and forge ahead. I try again—"How's it going?"—hoping to project myself as relaxed, confident, fearless.

Ten yards away the lead kid finally cracks. "What are you doing, taking pictures?"

I nod: "Yeah."

He says, "It's pretty out here," and strides right at me. I step aside, every muscle tensed . . . and they walk on by.

Puzzled, I turn with them, thinking: what the hell are they going to do, go stand in the middle of my landscape so I can't shoot a picture?

At an old prairie dog hole they brush away a tumbleweed; the teenager with the bota leans down and reaches inside. He locates a pair of one-way sunglasses, which he quickly fits over his eyes. The other kid laughs. They punch each other and giggle. Then head back toward me, suddenly animated, ready with an explanation.

"We were here yesterday, catching cottontails by hand. You seen any around?"

"Not many. One hightailed it up the gully when I arrived. It disappeared into the rocks over there. How do you catch them with your hands?"

"We just watch where they hide, then go and turn over the rocks and kill them with stones."

They are very friendly. Yesterday they wasted four rabbits. Good eating, too. And lost those sunglasses. Rabbits are so stupid, they have no trouble killing them by hand. Did it all the time.

Then they glance around, remarking again that it sure is a pretty evening, and skid down the embankment. They tumble a few rocks, hunting the rabbit I saw, but find nothing.

A few minutes later, still guzzling from the bota, tripping over their own feet and laughing, they reach their truck and depart. Gradually, my body quiets down. Relief comes; I feel very stupid for my paranoia. And I am determined to forget the vision I had of myself, sprawled by the Twin Rocks Puddle with a tiny bullet hole in my chest, undiscovered for weeks.

Years ago I bought a .22 pistol so that my children and I could fire blanks at the sky on New Year's Eve. Now I purchase real bullets for the weapon. And, on my next trip to the mesa, I slip the loaded gun into my camera pack.

A bitterness accompanies the act. Against my will I've been forced into another of America's cynical rites of passage.

FIFTEEN

C assandra teaches at an alternate school in Taos, a sort of Montessori-like establishment. She has read some of my books, and likes best *The Magic Journey*. On another Saturday, we are driving west to the mesa. While passing the Taos airport, she remarks on the push to lengthen its runways so that commercial jets may land, yet one more attempt to accelerate the valley's growth.

"Growth for the sake of growth," she says bitterly, "is the ideology of the cancer cell."

At the High Bridge spanning the river a new sign has gone up recently, advising tourists not to throw objects into the gorge. RAFTERS BELOW, warns the sign. Violators will be fined or imprisoned, or both.

Though I don't sympathize with rafters, I favor the sign. For I love to climb down a bajada just south of the bridge and fly fish up the riffles beneath the span. Too often, during these idylls, I have been bombarded by rocks and other lethal objects released by idiots overhead who think it's funny to threaten my life.

Years ago, I tell Cassandra, I usually had the Rio Grande to myself. But nowadays (at least during highwater times), the rafters have taken over. Some days it's a Coney Island of bright rubber and Coors-guzzling tourists on the water. "Needless to say, the mystique of the gorge takes a real licking."

According to Cassandra, "Anybody who kills a wild thing deserves to get inundated by rafters."

"What are you," I blast back scornfully, "a hippy-dippy

117

vegetarian?"

We laugh as I turn left onto the Carson Road, but I find that I am nervous in a new way with this big and coarsely beautiful woman.

A half mile later, in unison, we both exclaim: "Oh *NO!*" And once again I brake the Dodge in astonishment. We descend, and, circling the truck, I join Cassandra at the latest mesa shrine, a Day-Glo red and black tin plate slogan only a trifle less sacred than "In God We Trust":

NO TRESPASSING
This means you!

For emphasis, beneath the words a painted hand is pointing at *us*.

The absurdity is heightened by a hundred square miles of flat and unfenced sagebrush surrounding the sign. It's almost like a NO TRESPASSING sign in the middle of the ocean . . . or up in the sky!

Steaming mad—"I *hate* private property!"—Cassandra storms back to the truck. I follow, watching her long skirt flounce angrily against her ample rump. And my heart quickens for not exactly morally-outraged reasons.

All *kinds* of conflicting tensions are beginning to ripple across the placid mesa.

At the Sheep Corral Overlook we bite into cheese and tomato sandwiches, pop open Lite beers from Millers, and talk away the afternoon. Cassandra has spent time in Europe, and, years ago, she traveled with a Venceremos Brigade to Cuba.

"That really changed my life. God, what a different society! People there had such a lucid idea of their communal destiny. They had a really sophisticated historical perspective you rarely come across in this country. Clearly, they were all working together, and all terribly excited about the future. They were so *hopeful*. I couldn't get over that. Talk about poverty—they had almost nothing, yet they were so positive about life and about their revolution. I couldn't find any of the self-centered alienation that's so prevalent here."

We talk about Cuba, Mexico, the Soviet Union. I reminisce about a 1964 trip to Guatemala that shattered my illusions about America, the Big Benign Superpower. "Guatemala was such a miserable country. And how they hated us for the way we controlled them. As soon as I returned home I began to protest the Vietnam War."

The afternoon is exquisitely tranquil. I am happy, also a bit edgy about our proximity. Snow is sprinkled across the highest peaks and ridges of the Sangre de Cristos. Cassandra is scornful about the overlook, "It's absurd! It's almost stupidly beautiful!" And she turns on me: "Look, just don't start mouthing aesthetics at me, all right? The wretched of the earth need food, jobs, housing, medicine, not beautiful sunsets. I know most everybody at our meetings, maybe even you too, want to protect the lousy view out here—well, about that I don't give a damn. People come first, and I wouldn't be raising a fuss if I didn't believe that in the long run the people of this valley are gonna get screwed."

"There's just one thing I don't understand."

"What's that?"

"Would you like me to start mouthing aesthetics at you?"

She punches my shoulder hard—"Ouch!" This woman is *strong* (and Rubenesque . . . and even sultry, if only she would let down her guard for a moment).

Gazing into the majestic gorge, we discuss the world. My recent trip to Nicaragua comes up; I talk about my speeches since. Listeners are surprised I wasn't killed down there, astonished that I think it's a wonderful revolution. In return, Cassandra describes three months she spent in Managua, shortly after the 1979 insurrection, helping to plan the literacy campaigns.

(I picture her in the jungle, sleeves rolled up, sweat trickling between her breasts, a machete in one hand. And the powerful sculpted women of Gaston Lachaise cross my mind.)

Back and forth we go as the sun curves toward the southwest horizon. It is rare for either of us to find like-minded souls in Taos. We recall books by Eduardo Galeano, Ernesto Cardenal, Meg Randall, and Joseph Collins. We share a delight in Pablo Neruda, Marge Piercy, Otto René Castillo, and Walter Lowenfels. Through our animated conversation pass Nora Astorga and Carlos Fonseca, Victor Jara and Tina Modotti.

A vulture slides by as our topics rise and fall, change, recede, expand. I grow a bit woozy from sensual expectation. We agree that the destruction of the planet in World War II may pale in comparison to the violence done each year in the name of progress. We both understand that chemicals and intensive cash crop production have almost destroyed the fertile topsoil of American farmland. We know that in just a few years twenty percent of the Amazon has been destroyed. And sulpher dioxide emitted by southwestern smelters and power plants is increasing the acidity of Rocky Mountain lakes, so that shortly they'll begin to die off from the acid rain that has already killed six percent of New York's Adirondack ponds and twenty percent of Sweden's lakes.

Cassandra tells me, "I read in a paper the other day that ninety-seven percent of Michigan's inhabitants have been contaminated by the toxic chemical PBB."

"I read in the paper just last week that every *day* a hundred species go extinct."

"Every *day*, are you certain?"

"I think so. Or is it every week?" I hesitate. "Could it be every *year*—?" Our eyes meet and lock briefly; I flicker mine away.

We cavil against an economic system—ours—based on Planned Obsolescence and Conspicuous Consumption. Such a philosophy assumes that resources are infinite, and it is obviously a formula for planetary suicide.

We are like kids, perched on that overhang, confirming each other's correctness of vision. And secretly I keep wondering: *when* are we going to get to the *point*?

"That's one thing I loved about Nicaragua," I say. "Up

here there's so little support for my beliefs. I walk around feeling like an alien all the time. Then suddenly, down there, I'm in this laid-back, humorous, tough-as-nails little country where even the average man on the street can relate to my politics. It blew me away."

Neither of us wants the afternoon to end. We drag it out, discussing ways to change America, save the earth. Phase out automobiles, phase in public transportation. Shift populations out of cities, distribute them more evenly in the countryside. Develop solar energy and smaller, decentralized, more organic farming. Reduce American waste and luxury and economic imperialism so that the world's have-nots can begin to live better lives. Struggle for socialized medicine, abortion on demand, viable education, and an end to racism as an institutional tool for maintaining class divisions.

We feel that television, used properly, could make us literate again, teach us about the world, bring hundreds of other cultures into our lives, give all Americans in-depth historical, social, emotional perspectives.

"It could be so simple," Cassandra murmurs. "Today we're all taught to covet Jaguars, Chrysler Imperials, Honda motorbikes. Tomorrow we could learn to want an education, hate pollution, discover gardening, quit smoking. Through free TV courses we could all graduate college, learn to speak several languages . . ."

Je veux t'embrasser, comes to mind. And: *Te quiero, niña hermosa.*

Our dialogue doesn't end until after dark. We are both exhausted and exhilarated. The world is threatened, the world is a slaughterhouse, the world is no fun for most people. And, yes, it is also a beautiful, fascinating, worthwhile (and often erotic) adventure. The struggle for the future is all important; we both swear never to give up hope.

We are seated on a narrow rock ledge, inches from a precipice falling three hundred feet to a slope of talus boulders rumbling, without sound, down to the Rio Grande. Above us, the sky is brilliant with stars.

Gazing dreamily at Picuris Peak, I finally muster the courage to tell her: "I think I'm beginning to like you a lot."

Cassandra leans over, gently kissing my lips as she whispers tauntingly: "Well, Mr. Nichols—you be careful with your heart now, hear?"

Then she is up, stretching, yawning, laughing delightedly. "Okay, everybody—time to pack up and ride out. Robert will be screaming for supper."

I hate the little bugger already!

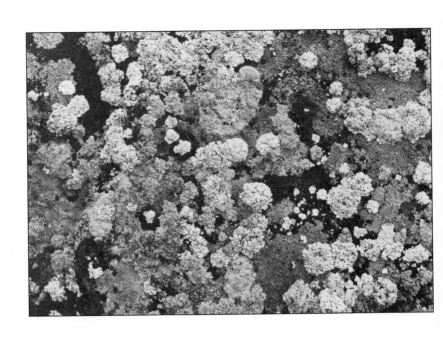

SIXTEEN

Time for a pilgrimage to the Lichen Rock.
I must admit to ulterior motives. This beautiful stone would look quite handsome greeting visitors in front of my house across the gorge.

And besides: winter is almost here. Won't be long now before the mesa shuts down, the roads become impassable, the cold grows intolerable, and I'll have lost my stomping grounds for a while. Yet with that rock constantly in view, reminding me of the mesa, I might feel less bereft.

Plus, in my gloomier moments I fear that Bill Bones, the power lines and company will smash the rock, destroy the pond, and devastate the mesa, so why not grab all I can get before the onslaught?

Against all the regulations and ethics of conservationists, then, I decide to snatch the rock. Who'll ever know the difference? Maybe I'll return it after the spring thaw.

Kneeling before the rock, I groove on its intricate colorful patterns. Shaped like a pig, it's only a foot and a half tall, maybe two feet wide; it rests on other stones. Step back ten yards, and it merges into the mesa's monotone. But up close its flamboyant patterns are riotous and wonderful.

While balanced on my haunches I remember that the primeval lichen combines an alga and a fungus. Its role is to secrete acids that gradually dissolve and decompose boulders, which crumble into earth. In time the lichens also die, joining the mineral crumbs they've loosened, further enriching the new soil. For some quirky reason (no doubt scientifically incorrect) I think of lichens as one of nature's bizarre little hermaphrodites.

Even as I hunker before them, the lichens are slowly eating this prosaic boulder. They chew their food awhile before digesting it. How long will it take them, noshing night and day, to create a single ounce of earth—eight thousand years? How long, already, has this poor stone been under such relentless attack by the aggressive lichens? Since the earth cooled? For ten thousand uneventful centuries? Or for only a mere dozen millenniums?

Should I weigh and measure the stone right now, return when I'm eighty, and calculate their rate of progress?

Mesa winds always blow toward the northeast mountains. Lichens cling to the north face of the rock; the south side is bare. If I cart home the stone, will the changed environment kill the lichens? To what extent do they depend for survival on the unique weather patterns of the arid plain?

Figuring I better expose some film before lugging off this treasure, I set up my tripod, take a meter reading, focus the lens, make all the necessary adjustments, and peek through the viewfinder: a skinny brown and white puppy occupies the right side of my picture. She pricks up her ears inquisitively. Angrily, I tell the dog to bug off, I'm doing art. She whimpers, wags her tail, refuses to budge. "Take a powder, mutt," I demand. She assumes an obsequious pose, and starts begging for friendship with ingratiating whines and pathetic moans.

Unnerved, in no mood to adopt a pet, I wing a few small stones at the unctious creature. Tail between her legs, she slinks away to safety, sits down, and yowls. Because she's still messing up the picture, I hurl a few more stones and several epithets. In due course, the puppy skulks out of frame.

But it's tough to wallow in erudite naturalist aesthetics with that gangly mutt whimpering in the background. Where does she hail from? No doubt she was dumped by a heartless master with no room for bitch puppies in his household—I don't blame him. Or could the dog be some sort of wilderness guardian, sent to protect a cherished landmark from my pilfering intentions?

Well, I take some photographs. And when the documentation of the Lichen Rock in its natural habitat is complete, I stow my paraphernalia and tackle the stone itself. The Dodge is a half mile away: this should be a piece of cake. I squat, get a solid grip, and lift—the rock doesn't budge. It's barely larger than a basketball, yet it must have a core of lead.

Twenty yards away, the puppy rocks back on her haunches and really wails, as if I were trying to rob the mesa of its very soul!

And, feeling foolish, I give up. What a dumb plan, anyway. Out of curiosity, I tilt the rock slightly and discover the jawbone of a small rodent underneath, a talisman I don't mind pocketing and adding to my mesa medicine bundle at home. But as I move on to other adventures, she—of the pandering eyes and deferential mien—follows, begging me with plaintive snivels, blubbers, and gurgles to rescue her from the desolate mesa, take her home, give her a warm hearth to sleep on.

No, *niechevo, nyet*, no thanks! At home I have a pet cat, *period*. His name is Duke. He's all black, weighs sixteen pounds, and is thoroughly independent. Neither of us violates the other's solitude. We don't need a frisky, yawping, flea-bitten moron cavorting noisily through our privacy. And besides, I travel too much. When I gather up more stones, sticks, and other warlike tokens, the pup retreats to the outer edge of my throwing range and uncorks some real wolf-like doozies.

Disgruntled, I wander over to a thistle patch. The puppy, whom I ignore, follows at a distance, occasionally pausing to release yet another grief-stricken yowl. I photograph a lovely tangle of lace-like branches. The dog locates a rotting foreleg and noisily chews it to pieces.

Pretty soon, I head for my vehicle. The puppy's dolorous lament dogs my heels. At the truck I grimly stash my gear, flip the ignition switch, and prepare to retreat. Off a ways the miserable bitch sits in a funereal posture; paint her face like a clown and stick a tear on her cheek and she would look perfect!

My motor roaring to life is obviously a death knell to the pathetic creature. Her gaze seems to ask: what sort of Nazi would trundle off cold turkey, leaving a cute little bundle of affection like her to the mercy of the cruel elements? I relent, set the handbrake, open the door, call the puppy. Coyly, she cocks her head: "Who *me*?" I growl, "Come on, hurry up, I ain't got all day." She rises, assumes an ultra-irritating obsequious timidity, and slinks over. At the passenger door she cowers, refusing to enter. Finally, I have to lift her up and in. I come away plastered with mud off her four huge paws.

Home we go. I feed the puppy, name her Jennifer, place an ad in the paper, nobody answers. Jenny gulps down a hundred pounds of dog food in seven minutes, then playfully jumps on Duke. He responds by almost tearing her head off, and her shrieks, as she tumbles away from his sharp claws, nearly pierce my eardrums.

It can only get worse. I ferry her to the vet for shots. She vomits ten pounds of Purina Puppy Chow all over the newspaper, two sacks of groceries, and my camera bag. Back home she camps forlornly on the portal whining to come inside. But we've decided she's an "outdoors dog." I make a straw-bale igloo for her on the portal and keep the kitchen door locked. Temperatures drop at night: in the morning Jenny's bruised eyes accuse me of heartlessness. Naturally, unable to deal with the guilt, I soon allow her in.

A mistake. Immediately Jennifer takes over. Duke retreats to the top of the fridge and pouts, surly and resentful. Jenny chews up some books, eats a camera case, and scars my good boots, slippers, and sneakers. I give her old sneakers to teethe on; but she only enjoys mint-condition leather Nikes.

All over town I post signs: *Please* take my adorable dog. So cute, so frisky, such a sweet personality. (She also demands ceaseless attention, she stinks, she's got fleas, she'll come into heat pretty soon, and she loves to roll in mud and putrid animal carcasses.) It's like having a two-year-old baby again.

Eventually—God bless!—a woman telephones in

response to one of my posters: it's Cassandra.

"Is the dog a revolutionary mutt?" she asks.

"Used to belong to Ché Guevara," I swear.

She and her small child, Robert, arrive to interview Jennifer. Jennifer happily knocks down the kid and slobbers all over him. "I like that," says Cassandra. "She's got spunk, she's not afraid to kick ass." Robert twists one of Jennifer's ears and the dog almost rips his nose off—he starts bawling.

No matter, they'll *take* Jenny but cannot fetch her for two more weeks. Cassandra is quitting her teaching job and must travel off to negotiate something vague with an ex-husband or ex-lover—she doesn't elaborate. I find her secrecy a trifle annoying, but no matter: Jennifer is the problem today. And, with relief in sight, Duke and I can handle anything.

Spontaneously, I hug Cassandra; surprisingly, she hugs me back. We hold it a little longer than the curious propriety set up between us dictates; then Robert kicks me in the shins: "Let's *go*, Mom!"

Next day Jenny busts her foot. Off to the vet again—more Purina puppy vomit all over the pickup cab. A hundred bucks takes care of x-rays, splints, shots, a cast. She promptly gnaws off the cast. Gotta worm her, too. Jenny devours tons of horse manure daily; she scratches on the door at night with animal dung literally dripping off her whiskers.

It arrives—the blessed day when Jenny will be transferred to her new masters (we hope, we pray). On that morning comes a blizzard. You can't see five feet ahead. And I realize it's hopeless, I'm stuck with the mutt. Then, through the whirling snow I spot Cassandra's Chevy rattletrap jolting up the driveway: *they've come!*

Neither Duke nor I can believe it. We rush outside, greet 'em warmly, toss Jennifer's straw-bale igloo into the truck, and hand over two boxes of Bonz, a carton of Milk Bones, a fifty-pound sack of Purina Puppy Chow, a small rubber mouse (that squeaks), and three thoroughly-chewed sneakers. Jennifer knocks down Robert, giving him a bloody nose; Cassandra hands Robert a Milk Bone to shut him up. I'm terrified this

latest incident will make them change their minds. But no—
Cassandra only tarries for a friendly cup of tea. We talk about
energy ripoffs in America, the Iran-Iraq war, Reagan's gathering debacle in Central America, and Wayne Gretzky. Turns out
Cassandra played ice hockey in prep school (Miss Halls) and
college (Radcliffe).

"So why is a preppy like you spouting all this seditious
bullshit?" I ask.

"Revolutions are always organized by the intellectuals,"
she teases. And as her truck maneuvers edgily back down the
potholed drive, removing Jennifer from our lives, Duke rubs
up against my leg, purring for the first time in weeks.

Ten minutes later the blizzard ends: all the snow is melted
by noon. And quiet permeates our household again.

Next time I have an impulse to steal a precious landmark
from the mesa, I'll count to ten, turn in circles, bite my contrite
tongue, and trundle off in another direction.

So the Lichen Rock remains where it has always been,
unnoticed by everything and everyone except me, slowly but
surely being devoured by hermaphrodites.

Certain apprehensions color my next few mesa visits. Suppose Jennifer wasn't punishment enough for my near-
transgression? Other retributions could be in store. One in
particular I might anticipate is an old classic for this sort of terrain: the Rattlesnake Bite.

So far, in years of wandering, I've encountered few snakes.
I recall one, fourteen years ago, on the road ten miles south of
the stock pond. And in 1980 I almost stepped on a rattler in the
bottom of a dry reservoir west of Tres Orejas. That same year,
halfway up the three-eared mountain, I ran into a mess of
snakes near a blowhole where they'd been wintering. But to
date I have never disturbed a rattler near the stock pond.

Nevertheless, now that I'm feeling a trifle sheepish about
my karma, I keep an especially wary eye out, just in case. It
seems past their denning time . . . but you never can tell.

Which immediately creates a self-fulfilling prophecy, i.e., being extra aware of the devil, the devil promptly appears.

I discover this rattler in much the same manner I usually meet them. That is, I almost step on it near the Twin Rocks Rain Puddle. My eyes are feasting on some twilight cumulus lunacy over Cerro Peak when somehow I sense the snake, manage to twist in mid-air and shuffle-hop sideways, and don't quite break my ankle. And though my heart almost leaps out through my sternum, then flutters wildly, triggering a tingling icy sweat, it stops just short of a major attack. Pretty soon I gather my wits and take a closer look at my venomous friend.

This one is barely eighteen inches long. Had I stepped on it the snake would have been royally squashed. No doubt positively paralyzed from fear itself, the rattler makes no move to escape. Although I was brought up to understand that snakes always give a warning, I've since learned that is hogwash: they almost never rattle. Probably they have adopted this caution with humans because nine times out of ten a person, on encountering any serpent, will hack, chop, bash, kick, slice, and otherwise torment it immediately. Hence, rattlesnake survival in habitats frequented by people depends on keeping a real low profile.

Rattlesnakes are important to me. They give lustre to the mesa. Granted, cows have a certain prairie mystique; and wild horses give romance to pale indigo ranges. Prairie dogs add reliable comic relief to Hollywood westerns. And the coyote is a cunning rascal no mesa could do without. But it's the near-sighted, beautiful rattlesnakes who provide a sweet element of danger, and solidify my respect for the high country flatlands.

So: there I am, a bit weak-kneed, wondering how to photograph the snake on ASA 25 film in such dim light. And the rattler? It doesn't move. I'm sure the reptile has already factored in all available information, and is fairly cognizant of the survival odds, should a contretemps between us develop.

Therefore, I'm in no danger unless I do something very stupid.

I snap a few pictures, then sit down and regard the quiet snake, who remains coiled against a rock from which sunshine is softly leaking. No expansions or contractions of the snake's body indicate that it's breathing. Rarely in nature have I seen a critter remain so immobile. Finally, a little impatiently, I pick up a stick and give a poke. The sensation of the snake through that stick is curious: like a hollow, raspy thing . . . like worn, dry shoe leather wrapped around an empty space—

In your typical Blinding Instant, the snake whirls, ready to strike; prudently, I remove my hand—almost tipping over backwards. Golly—that was *fast!* My heart revs up again; I almost faint. But the urge passes, and we both settle down. The snake rests its chin on a fat coil, attending my next move.

I choose to do little but inspect the small rattler. Its beige-green skin seems moist, radiant. With the stick I cautiously rub a coil. This time the serpent barely flinches. Clearly, it doesn't want to strike. Our agreement is one of mutual respect—live and let live.

Soporific calm spreads. The snake's black bifid tongue emerges at intervals, keeping track of my bulk, my body warmth, my smell. Though deaf, rattlesnakes are sensitive to ground vibrations. They have a short, and not very articulate range of vision, say fifteen or twenty feet. The indentations, or pits behind their eyes are temperature differential receptors, and they can "see," or locate, nearby things quite well with these thermoreceptive sensors. But the tongue is apparently the snake's most highly developed sense apparatus. It's a chemoreceptor which conveys particles from the air into two pits on the roof of the mouth called Jacobson's Organs. Instantly (in thirty-five milliseconds) the organs analyze the data and pass it on to the brain. What the brain of this snake is saying right now I can only guess. Probably, "Lay low, bro', you're in trouble: this dude weighs 175 pounds!"

At each appearance the tongue first curls under the chin, then it flips up and backwards over the head, lying down flat against the forehead. Then—*slurp*—it retreats back inside. Again and again–the only motion between us. I understand now that these odd tongue movements are also intended to threaten.

Darkness settles. When I touch the rattler a last time there's a scraping sound, a kind of dusty and thick echo, as if the snake were both heavy and weightless. Per usual, the Tres Orejas coyotes fire off a rabble-rousing blood-curdle—and then fall silent.

How small and vulnerable is the creature before me, curled up in primitive loneliness; it really doesn't stand much of a chance, does it?

We part company; I trudge off. The night air is frosty. Too chilly for the rattler? I wonder. Did my interruption keep it from finding a warm refuge in time to save itself? If a freeze hits, will the snake be dead by morning—?

SEVENTEEN

A bout a week before the mesa committee's fund raiser, I return from a short hop to the West Coast and begin organizing slides for my presentation. Bearing a bottle of Jack Daniels Black Label, Cassandra pops in one evening to kibitz at the selection process. Little Robert and bouncing Jennifer also descend, much to the chagrin of Duke, who retreats to a cardboard box (in my closet) full of tax receipts. I hand everyone a pair of chopsticks and a bowl of my patented Garden Goulash, then Cassandra and I go to work.

Funny thing about taking pictures. When slides first return from Kodak and I breeze through them in a hand viewer, I'm ecstatic. "Move over Ansel Adams, Ed Weston, Laura Gilpin!" Then I dump them in a carrousel, set up a screen, and begin to have second thoughts: magnified flaws leap out like Barishnykov. From every packet of thirty-six shots, I soon discard at least twenty-five. The survivors I stack in carrousels atop my gutted player piano, and try not to dwell on my incompetence as a cameraman.

But introduce another person into the viewing process, and it gets downright rough. I shrivel inside; my skin crawls. I can't believe I'm such an amateur. I'm embarrassed, queasy, humiliated. I want to toss it all in the garbage, apologize profusely for being such an arrogant schmuck, and make up excuses: asthma, bad heart, Méniére's disease, I drink too much, double vision, color blindness, numismatic dermatosis—

"Wait a minute, whoa, not so *fast!*" cries Cassandra.

"Lemme see that last slide again."

All asquirm, I punch back the former slide: "Look, I know it's not very interesting. There's a Newton ring. I don't know what I was thinking—"

"Oh shuttup, please. Just let me *look* at it for a minute without your damn morose voice slobbering all over me."

Cassandra squints, assessing. I twitch, lick my parched lips, rub a palm across my eyes, tear my hair, grimace, jiggle both legs, wish I was in Cozumel.

"You're right," she finally admits. "It stinks. That Isaac Newton thing screws up the balance. Plus, you know, the whole concept is out of whack. Next."

"Oh—?" Eyebrow arched, head cocked, I piercingly evaluate the photograph. Incredibly, of a sudden it looks rather beautiful. I'm a trifle hurt. I explain, "You always see Newton rings in a picture like this. It helps to accent that glare effect. Of course, it may not be a great *technical* photograph, but I think it's sort of refreshing, ingenuous, understated, *natural*. There's no gimmick to the shot; the camera doesn't intrude; it just records exactly what's there. Don't you think it captures one of the mesa's more profound moods?"

"Okay." She nods too quickly, too agreeably. "Then include it."

Instantly, second thoughts. "Well, I don't know if it's *that* good. I mean, let's not go overboard. You're probably right about the 'off-balance' part—"

Why do I feel sick to my stomach? On earth, can there be a more fatuous artistic dilettante than me?

"Well, so fine," says Ms. Cheerful. "*Don't* include it. If I were you, I'd trust my own shit detector, nobody else's. Next picture, please." When nothing happens, her head swivels, her large blue eyes glance up. "What's the matter?"

"I don't know if I'd rather strangle you—" I mutter darkly, "—or hang myself!"

A sobbing Robert lands on the living room doorstep, and he puts everything—art, politics, human relationships—into perspective:

"Mom, Jennifer ate all my fucking goulash!"

With the help of Jack Daniels, we make it through the night. And come the hour of our fund raiser, I've got a carrousel of mouth-watering slides ready to speak for the mesa.

Don't ask why, but our event is staged in the Cafe Tazza, a fine place to eat tamales and drink cappuccino, but not the largest joint in the world. Maybe twenty of us, arranged sideways sardine-style, can cram into the gallery-meeting room side of the establishment. Others dawdle outside or among tea tables in the west wing. Most onlookers are friends or members of our Committee to Save the Mesa: not a sympathetic millionaire glitters in the bunch. Obviously, we're preaching to the already-converted, most of whom also qualify as the heartily non-rich. No wherewithal for a legal defense fund will accumulate at this get-together. Nevertheless, our show must go on.

Comes my turn, I click jauntily through the slides, and pontificate about the mesa. I mention the stock pond, the avocets and phalaropes, the sage terrain and Tres Orejas, my admiration for rattlesnakes. As the carrousel turns, I realize anew how very deeply I care for the mesa. Shared with others, the photographs heighten my desire to protect the freedom of that space.

Toward the end, a slide focuses on Tres Orejas. I speak warmly of expeditions on the mountain. I mention the nest of eagles.

"Hey, man, don't be telling people about those eagles!" An artist friend rises angrily. "You tell them about eagles, next thing you know, every asshole in Taos will be over there with binoculars and cameras and beer bottles, and probably even stinking *chain saws*, and the eagles will split in a minute. Christ, keep your mouth shut about those eagles, John."

"Oh hey, people already know about the eagles, and—"

"Maybe they do, maybe they don't, but sure as hell if you go around advertising the mesa, putting a bunch of pretty pictures in a book, you'll create a stampede over there, just like some of your other stuff! Like *The Milagro Beanfield War* or *The Last Beautiful Days Of Autumn* have brought all kinds of riffraff in to destroy this valley."

And he sits down with a mighty defiant harrumph.

Taken by surprise, I don't know how to react. An emotional comeback is pointless. I click to another slide: "These are the tracks of horned larks on the fresh snow, eating Russian thistle seeds—"

"Horned larks, fine, talk all you want," my friend growls, folding arms across his barrel chest. "Who cares about horned larks?—dime a dozen. Just please do us all a favor and lay off the poor eagles."

An irate woman shakes her fist at him: "Sir, *I* care about horned larks!"

"Good!" he snaps. "Then *you* worry about the horned larks, ma'am, and *I'll* worry about the eagles!"

A reporter from an Albuquerque TV station awaits us in the courtyard after the show. Dumping all the equipment in Cassandra's arms, I prepare to be interviewed. The reporter, a high-strung blond woman, says I'll have approximately thirty seconds to give my answer. "Okay—what is the question?"

"Why is it that you're opposed to powerlines and other development on the mesa?"

Every now and then, right in the middle of a speech, or a conversation, or an interview, something goes "click!" in my brain, and I draw a blank. And right now, with my lips two inches from a hand-held mike, and a chance to strike a statewide blow for the mesa, I turn into a quivering deaf-mute with a whitewashed brain.

"Um . . . uh . . . well . . . I . . . sure . . . I mean . . ."

Cassandra leans over and snaps out a statement as sharply as if it were poised at the tip of a cracking bull whip.

"He's against it because it's a project that will cost the public an arm and a leg, and provide excess electricity nobody can use. Yet the people in Taos County, a majority of whom are very poor, will have to pay for that useless electricity without receiving any benefits from it. And even if there is finally some growth, and the price goes down, that growth—if the past is any indication—will only benefit people on the top part of the economic scale. The working class of Taos County—already poorer, in terms of their actual dollar buying power, than they were in 1950—will just get more destitute. Believe us, they don't buy *more* security lamps, washing machines, freezers, or VCRs—they can't afford them in the first place! Not only that, but the path chosen by the unneeded transmission lines will ruin the grazing lands and stock ponds of several marginal ranchers on the mesa, whose language, culture, and ethics are important to this valley. Also, the transmission lines will effectively destroy one of the last wild areas in Taos, illegally infringe upon the congressional mandate of the Rio Grande's Wild River Section, and, by so destroying the attractive environment of Taos, wind up adversely affecting still another of our already shaky tourist-oriented economic foundations."

Period. Amen.

The reporter addresses me: "Mr. Nichols, are those your sentiments also?"

I nod vigorously. "Yup. That's it exactly. In a nutshell . . ."

"What *happened* to you?" Cassandra asks in the car going home. "Were you having a fibrillation?"

"No, I think I was just terrified I'd say something about the eagles, and that artist guy would see it on TV and come over and drive his jeep at sixty miles an hour into my living room while I'm watching the Edmonton Oilers in the seventh game of the Stanley Cup finals."

"Mom," Robert wheedles from the back seat of my '73 Chevy Impala: "Jennifer just upchucked all over the slide projector!"

At home I scrub clean the projector and the slide carrousel, and stack them atop my old piano. Then, slouching tiredly on the stool, I tinker with the dirty ivories, whispering phrases of a laconic blues tune. Cassandra deposits Robert on the couch; he flakes out immediately. Then she drifts over and settles by my side, draping an arm around one shoulder. I continue puttering, flushing a bit from her warmth, the faint smell of her hair and rumpled clothes. How odd to know a woman like this, so intimate in certain ways, so remote and unapproachable in others. I still have no idea how to move closer, suggesting a physical get-together. Our connection is intriguing, mysterious, frustrating—I can't read her at all.

So I remain hunched on the stool, quietly playing an old Michael Murphey song, "Calico Silver"—it touches my heart every time I remember the tune.

Cassandra finally leans close and nibbles on my ear: "I'm pooped, my friend. Can Robert and I crash here tonight?"

"Sure. Whatever you want."

"Okay—but on one condition."

"Namely—?" I play G, then A7, then D7.

"I think it's time for us to make love."

I hesitate but half a moment: then I play F, Em, and C.

EIGHTEEN

A moment ago the mesa was flourishing. Now it is withered again . . . or all gone underground.

Winter keeps approaching; the landscape is increasingly stark. Nearly finished are the bird migrations. Rain quits falling altogether. Bleak yet soft are the shortening days. Sunshine drapes thinly over impervious sage. Rocks stay cold all day.

A mere puddle remains where once stood the teeming stock pond. A deserted air frames the mood; animals tunnel still deeper. Prairie dogs no longer stand noisy watch on the rims of their hills. Ants have gone dormant beneath their pebble cones. I cease being alert for rattlesnakes.

On evenings for a week a lone nighthawk quarters the air over the stock pond, hunting penultimate insects. Then the discouraged bird gives up, travels south. A single bat feeds over the small reservoir in which the evening star is reflected—pickings must be slim. If ice formed now, I could only stand still on the tiny pond: in motion I'd have to turn every two strokes; I'd be dizzy and nauseous in a minute.

The season winds down further. Swallows departed the Gorge Overlook long ago. Three A.M. winds tear apart the ring muhly fields; next morning a barely-frozen stock pond is rimmed in golden grasses. Later on that cold sunny day I spot a rare bald eagle circling above the gorge. Snow inches down toward the base of the mountains; it piles deeper on the summits. Dove season ended a month ago. Surviving deer and elk are safe until next year. Killdeer cries no longer reverberate over the tranquil mesa.

Ski season begins across the gorge. From my isolated post on the dam, I catch the boom of avalanche control explosions. In the closer distance, I hear two different well drillers pounding casings down into the earth; it seems, suddenly, as if a regular village is sprouting against the foothills of Tres Orejas—landowners eagerly anticipating the boom.

Old pickup trucks full of dry piñon deepen the ruts on dirt roads. People are poaching wood around Tres Orejas, cutting lots of green trees. The Forest Service increases its surveillance; several leñeros without papers are arrested.

Late at night, somebody fells one of Bill Bones' Electric Cafe signs; but by the next afternoon he has it rebuilt and reinforced by steel plating. That night gallons of blue paint are splashed across the billboard. For two days it appears the eco-guerillas have triumphed. Then a new billboard pops up, complete with metal legs and an easily replaced polyurethane sheath protecting the message. We all hold our breaths—but the saboteurs appear disheartened.

"Bill Bones ain't your average run-of-the-mill wimp," says Bill Bones, quoted in a *Taos News* article. "GUNS, GUTS, AND GLORY— " reads his pickup's bumper sticker, "—ARE WHAT MADE AMERICA GREAT."

The Committee To Save The Mesa responds with its own bumper sticker: "WILL ROGERS NEVER MET BILL BONES."

Autumn wanes. I can almost jump over the stock pond. The clear sky seems faintly bruised. A melancholy settles over the land. Fresh earth around small burrows suggests the underground dwellers are preparing to bed down for a long haul. Winterfat seeds are scattered around these entrances: food-gathering never seems to end.

Days go by and not a single migrant lands at the stock pond. The Twin Rocks Rain Puddle evaporates entirely, taking with it the mosquitoes, water beetles, fairy shrimp. In the mornings, in the evenings, a band of haze from town wood fires lies along the eastern foothills. Russian thistles on the north rim of Coyote Gulch are dry and silvery. Hundreds of milkweed hair tufts, blown loose by the wind, are ensnared in thistle branches. At twilight the sunset touches them with fire.

A serious stillness overtakes the plateau. Now is the time of bones and feathers, of small talismans left behind—the residue of all the mesa's hasty aliveness.

At the dry Twin Rocks Puddle I wonder: how far did that small rattler travel to go denning? With an effort I raise a wide flat stone resting atop other rocks. In the shelter beneath are dry grasses molded into a nest, lots of rat (or toad, or gopher?) droppings, and an old snakeskin. Maybe my friend hung out here at night, in warmer times.

At the Sheep Corral Overlook, Cassandra finds another snakeskin, caught on the spines of prickly pears. No doubt shed weeks ago, how far was it blown to arrive at this place? She picks it up and places it carefully in the truck.

At the overlook I notice a white reflection deep in the crevace between two boulders. Reaching down, I grasp a small jackrabbit skull. For a while I inspect the brittle structure, fascinated by the winged shape of eye sockets, by the tiny teeth, by the intricate webbings of bone and the detailed zig-zagging cracks across the paper thin cranium. I could easily get lost in the study of elfin skulls. The craftsmanship in Lillipu-tian jawbones and miniature teeth seems so far beyond any artistic expression humans could invent. When I choose to look closely at anything—a skull, a dried flower, a snakeskin—its perfect complexity tunnels into my brain. The intricate symmetry of a rabbit skull can hold its own with the fantastic vaulted knaves of medieval cathedrals.

From the dying landscape I solicit feathers, bones, and other small recuerdos. A sheep skull and chunks of vertebrae lie near the bean pot in the Western Gully. I scrutinize a single disc of the spinal column. Its shape is as graceful as a bird, a tropical fish; no matter how I tilt it, the bone appears to be flying or swimming. It has a rudder on top (or on the bottom), a wing to either side, four streamlined hooks, an oddly wrinkled front and backside, an almond-shaped hole through the center. Though each part of this lovely structure must have a scientific name, I don't know it. I only know that I hold in my hand an amulet of singular beauty. To Cassandra it goes, on her birthday.

In several gullies are rib bones, slim and curved, quicksilver graceful, like wands fallen from the hands of invisible curanderas floating overhead. I sail one through the air, a lightweight boomerang, a skeletal feather. The elegant cleanliness of its lines is fluent and alluring. I run my finger along the chaste, curving length—so harmonious and classic.

Cassandra has a way with dreamy proclamations: "If we could polish our souls with bones, what a powerful simplicity might light up the world!"

Bones are complete, final, reassuring.

The jawbones, ribs, and other bleached knick knacks of a horse lie in a far arroyo, been there for years, undisturbed. Shards of a frayed halter rope melt into the loose soil. Wheat grass and muhly grow among the bones; sagebrush is there; smooth stones fill in some blank spaces.

Hunkering nearby, I speculate on the life and death of the horse, its final moments. Shot by a homesteader, killed by a blizzard, dragged down in decrepit old age by ravenous coyotes—? Perhaps tired, hungry, infested by parasites, numb from autumn frost, the enormous animal simply kneeled down to expire.

While giving my imagination rein, I finger the soil, picking up sticks and nubbin-sized stones, thoughtfully rolling them between my fingers. The feel of one object catches my interest; I inspect it more closely. By chance I have found an arrowhead. The tip is broken. It's made from a white stone, flecked with red dots.

Quietly amazed, I rub it between my thumb and forefinger. I have never found an arrowhead before.

On a dark night, horsebones reassemble and begin to dance, a muffled knick-knocking jangle beneath the clouds. Rabbit skeletons and coyote skulls prance irreverently beside the arroyos, mocking the timidity of ectoplasmic rattlesnakes caught in the shackles of melting terrain.

Bones have a tantalizing life of their own that goes beyond the simple enhancement of a Lonesome Sageland mystique.

Hollow sparrow bones, tangled in the hair of midnight winds, rarely settle to earth. Pneumatized skeletons of horned larks drift back and forth at human eye level like capricious dirigibles. Hawks, ravens, even little juncoes use bones scattered about the wide mesa as fixed points for navigating across monotonous landscapes. On Halloween a million ants awake and move the entire skeleton of a cow forty yards in seven hours. Wind strips off the last remnants of ligament ignored by the ants, ravens, and coyotes. In the process bones empty out . . . fill up with air . . . grow lighter, brighter, whiter.

Last August, a hummingbird traversing the wasteland at night grew so disoriented it fell to earth and was promptly stripped of feathers and flesh by dragonflies and carrion beetles. Now the miniscule clockwork parts of its skeleton, so tiny not even tweezers can pinch them, languidly drift about as if levitated by the gravity of stars many light-years away.

The aluminum-blue feather of a mountain bluebird is caught on the rough bark of a four-wing saltbush. In the dust below lies the jawbone of a baby lizard, a jewel perfect enough to squeeze a drop of wonder from even the most hardened horse thief.

A prairie dog skull is wide, flat, thicker than the rabbit skull I found at Sheep Corral Overlook. All the crannies of a coyote skull are packed with layered spider webbing. Some animal has chewed on the jawbone of a deer, whose tooth enamel remains remarkably polished. A small owl pellet contains the entire cranium of a mouse imbedded and preserved in compacted gray fur.

On Tres Orejas Mountain, below the eagle nest exposed by smears of white guano on the cliff face, are many castings of greasy fur harboring all kinds of small bones. Cassandra and I pry the pellets apart, carefully extricating the toenails of pocket gophers, the claws of prairie dogs, the delicate bone structure of complete mouse feet, flakes of skulls. For months, below the aerie, big white down feathers have been stuck to thorn bushes. I'd like to reach the deserted nest, but I have no climbing equipment, so it's too dangerous.

From the bottom of the cliff, hands on our hips, we gaze up at the crevice painted white from months of bird droppings, and try to imagine the daily lives of eagles, their fledglings, the beasts they hunted, ate, and disgorged.

Then, eyes closed, we picture the moment when all the raptors spread their wings together and sailed into the wild skies of an entire hemisphere.

Not far from the Sheep Corral Overlook, just below the rim of the gorge, is another aerie. A few times a year I check it out. It must be used by smaller hawks, for the bones are miniscule. Clinging to the edge of the cliff, I collect the bones; some I can barely pinch between my fat fingertips. Occasionally, I wet my finger and press bones onto it, then nudge them off into a match box. As always, I get high on the complexity of such smallness. The bones have many different shapes, all exquisite. They are porous, pneumatic, almost weightless—I bounce them in my palm like grains of sand. Hip bones, pelvic girdles, femurs, clavicles: thin as pins, fine as stiff thread. Cassandra pictures them as gems being reassembled under a jeweler's loupe. A hundred bones might fit in the space of her thumbnail, or displace the inner workings of an expensive Swiss watch.

"What sort of critters did they come from?" she asks. "Inch-long spadefoot toads? Or lizards and silky pocket mice?"

Consider the bone size and weight of some warm-blooded species, especially birds. Our smallest hummingbirds weigh a tenth of an ounce when alive; the enormous frigate bird, possessing a seven-foot wing span, has all its organs, muscles and feathers attached to a skeleton that only weighs four ounces! In my match-box are a hundred bones that might construct half a skeleton. Each bone is hardly more than a white splinter set in the center of my enormous fingertip whorls.

If butterflies or bumblebees had bones, here they'd lie, sticking to our skin. We are careful not to harm them as we collect them, for the smaller things get, the more their diaphanous complexity commands reverence.

A snake swallows a rabbit: all the bones dissolve, the fur does not. A kingsnake downs a rattlesnake: everything is digested except the rattles. Owls and eagles eat rabbits, lizards, and frogs: their acids dissolve all except bones, claws, and fur. Carrion beetles, ants, vultures, and the maggots of common flies pick clean the carcass of a sheep—only the bones remain. In due course, even those bones break down into a calcium powder that sifts into the porous earth, becoming a building block again.

Nothing ever leaves the world, or rises into the atmosphere but what it returns again. Human coffins strike me as grotesque, denying the only immortality we ever get. Why retard the disintegration of bones, teeth, fur, and scales, feathers, cartilage, and claws?—these things have built the layer of dirt and water and vegetation that girdles the globe and gives resilience to the air we breathe.

In my palm lies a half-inch-long bone shaped like a lacrosse stick. At the base of the triangular-shaped catching basket is a perfectly round socket, into which another sliver once fit perfectly. The handle-end of the stick is splayed, ridged on both sides, flared out thinly like an oar.

Cassandra exalts: "A mosquito could row across the galaxy with such a bone!"

NINETEEN

B efore you leave on your next movie junket, let's spend an entire night on the mesa." Cassandra is curling a lock of hair around the index finger of her left hand, while the right hand poises a Dos Equis beer bottle at her plump, unpainted lips.

"Okay."

It's spur of the moment, five P.M., almost dark—no time for fancy-schmancy. We dump a double mattress—all made up—into the bed of the Dodge, construct fat sandwiches, throw beer in a cooler and water into a gallon cider jug, toss in matches, instant coffee, a tea kettle, and old newspapers for starting a fire, then head for the Sheep Corral Overlook.

It's been one of those days. And it turns into one of those nights—languid and bland, so still and clear you're almost tempted to bring up religion. Almost. Prehistoric (and holy) is the mesa's peacefulness.

We gather dead sage branches, light a fire, eat sandwiches and drink beer, sip scalding coffee, and let our fire die, so that the night, with its grandiose profusion of electric baubles, can lower to what would be treetop level if trees existed on the mesa.

Unmoving, untalking, we mostly gaze at the dying flames. Night coils around us, full of sagebrush and smoke odors. Cassandra lights one cigarette a month, and chooses now to roll her own Bull Durham. Wonderful crisp light, billions of years old, shines on our shoulders. We luxuriate in hypnotic wooziness, elevating campfire-staring into high art. The embers warm only our faces: we don puffy jackets and knitted caps. My eartips and calves tingle from the cold. Still, our laziness makes it impossible to move. As the coals dim farther, the night expands around us, cool and bright. Why wrench our eyes away from surviving sparkles?—we are drugged, nearly catatonic, happy to float stupidly, without speaking, totally becalmed. A coyote on Tres Orejas cackles rapturously over some bedraggled bloody victim. And only when the last spark fizzles does Cassandra murmur a lazy phrase.

"Come again? I didn't hear you."

"I'm cold. And horny."

"Me too."

"Then what say we climb into the sack and haul each other's ashes?"

"I don't know if I've got the strength."

"Oh, you poor boy—"

Before I can cry "Help!" the husky woman stoops and grapples me up with a loud grunt, wrestles my 170 squirming pounds over to the truck, and shoves me over a gunwhale like a sack of potatoes, crucifying both patellas and a buttock.

Seconds later we're both gasping on our backs, muffled in a profusion of raunchy blankets and dirty goosedown, holding hands, confronting that old mysterious panoply of asteroids, white dwarfs, pale moons, and constellations known as The Universe.

And the last thing I remember, her lips are almost touching my mouth, and in her inches-distant eyes shimmer the haunting reflections of mesa constellations.

Three A.M. I awaken and quietly stare at the sky. Beside me, Cassandra dreams, her warm flesh aglow. I take her hand and peer aloft, thinking how only a few miles of atmosphere separate me from the impersonal expanse of an infinite universe. If I lifted my arm, I might poke a hole through that nebulous web of ozone, and feel, against the tip of my finger, a diamond-like chill as I touched outer space.

After a while, I begin to feel as if I'm floating in the radiant bubble of a blue universe. And I find myself fascinated by the brightly-polished moon shining peaceably in the lucid sky. Features of that distant lunar terrain seem to stand out clearly; for a moment I can almost distinguish individual craters . . . and the Sea of Tranquility. Soon I am intrigued by that deserted satellite, and interested in the fact that human beings once tramped upon its surface.

In fact, all at once a powerful envy churns through my guts. How I wish *I* could have looked upon the mesa from the pock-marked surface of the moon! What mysteries—of space, weather, humanity—might have been revealed, giving me fantastical insights with which to launch my imagination. It greatly disappoints me today that our men who touched the moon were not much given to flights of fancy, or to emotional outbursts. Technology they have revealed, says I . . . but not the human soul.

In 1973, the commander of the Apollo 15 moon landing wrote an article for *National Geographic* about his visit to the moon. David Scott remarked that the nightly reflections of sunlight off our earth illuminate the moon much more than the moon brightens our nights. He mentioned a stillness without wind, no sounds, only shadows moving. He was reassured by the constant purring of little motors in his space suit supplying oxygen, keeping him pressurized so he wouldn't explode, shielding him from the unbearable heat of the lunar morning.

Space is a vacuum, Scott explained, therefore on the moon there is very little decay. Even the footprints he left "in the undrifting dust" would acquire "a permanence akin to immortality."

To me the friendliest part of Scott's article was a short riff on falling down in the one-sixth gravity up there. "To fall on the moon—and I did several times—is to rediscover childhood. You go down in slow motion, the impact is slight, the risk of injury virtually nil. Forsaking the adult attitude that regards a fall not only as a loss of dignity but also a source of broken bones, the moon walker—like a child—accepts it as yet another diversion."

Something there touches my heart: to be a child on the moon. To float, to take a tumble, and land with no danger of pain. It's so close to flying, so reminiscent of childhood dreams, those long ago fantasies of invulnerability. The first thing I would have done, had I been chosen to land on the moon, would have been gracefully to leave my feet in order to experience that luxurious weightlessness as I tumbled toward the ground.

In fact, right now I feel powerfully in tune with the moon, as close as I may ever come to actually being there. The mesa is seductive and buoyant; gravity *is* less restricting out here. Often I seem to move through the sagebrush with an ease that formerly was only dreamed of in fairy tales.

My mind drifts all over the place. I am acutely alive. I'm aware of pure energy rippling out of my body and across the sage plateau. Complex electric circuits in rabbit brush branches are humming. Horned toads could move heaven and earth if they but understood how to exploit their tiny heartbeats. The breast feathers of a shrike could explode if touched with a magic consciousness. A different "holocaust" hums around me with not-necessarily-malevolent intent. Stars flickering beyond the moon utilize a fusion process similar to what happens in hydrogen bombs. All matter, the stuff of life, the benign material that composes this beautiful mesa, is bewilderingly *volatile*. The amount of plutonium actually fissioned to kill eighty thousand people at Nagasaki was one gram—or a third the weight of a penny!

What touches me most powerfully, as I lie on my back in the truck (holding sleeping Cassandra's hand), are my human connections to all the phenomena of aliveness . . . and those connections begin with the stars upon which my eyes are fixated.

According to Robert Jastrow: "A star is born out of the condensation of clouds of gaseous hydrogen in outer space. As gravity pulls together the atoms of the cloud, its temperature rises until the hydrogen nuclei within it begin to fuse and burn in a series of reactions, forming helium first, and then all the remaining substances of the universe. The elements of which our bodies are composed were manufactured in this way, in the interiors of stars now deceased, and distributed to space when these stars exploded."

Narrowing it down further, Vincent Cronin tells me that, "Our bodies contain three grams of iron, three grams of bright, silver-white magnesium, and smaller amounts of manganese and copper. Proportionate to size, they are among the weightiest atoms in our bodies, and they came from the same source, a long-ago star. There are pieces of star within us all."

Long before Cronin wrote those words, Walt Whitman exclaimed, "I believe a leaf of grass is no less than the journeywork of the stars!"

And in his book, *The Lives of a Cell*, Lewis Thomas has this to say about the connections: "The uniformity of the earth's life, more astonishing than its diversity, is accountable by the high probability that we derived, originally, from some single cell, fertilized in a bolt of lightning as the earth cooled. It is from the progeny of this parent cell that we take our looks; we still share genes around, and the resemblance of the enzymes of grasses to those of whales is a family resemblance."

"What are you thinking about?" Cassandra asks, wide awake.

"Connections."

"What sort of connections?"

"Cosmic. Universal. Human."

Squeezing my hand, she snuggles in tightly against my shoulder. "I have a favorite quote about all that."

"Spoken by—?"

"The naturalist, John Muir."

"And it is . . . ?"

"'When we try to pick out anything by itself, we find it hitched to everything else in the universe.'"

Nothing compares to a cloudless dawn on the mesa. Like the truly nuclear fireball it is, the sun rises and within moments the mesa is *hot*. Uncomfortably awash in perspiration, we awaken early, and groggily push off the rumpled bedclothes.

Side-by-side we lie under a blueness so vivid it threatens to drown us in unblemished purity. Eyes closed, hips and shoulders touching, we drowse along, letting the heat mollycoddle our cuts, bruises, throat hickeys. Opening one bloodshot eye, Cassandra lasciviously canvasses my southern latitudes and smirks, "Maybe we should hook a flag to it and pledge allegiance." *And why not?* I think, saturated in radiant sexual afterglow: *After a night like that, it may never wilt again!*

One thing leads to another, but just as the bells start ringing, a terrible highwhining roar shatters the quietude, and—both squealing—we snap upright just in time to face a military fighter jet blasting toward us along the edge of the gorge barely fifty feet above the sagebrush. Though my first thought is *It's a strafing run*, I can't duck for cover as the F-16 or the F-111 or whatever it is screams onward. For a split second the pilot is visible, his hand no doubt on the machine gun button—then, with a deafening screech the plane is a half-mile past us and already veering up in a northwest looping curve to swing back again, while its wake flattens the blankets, blows up our hair, and rattles hotly against our naked bodies.

The plane is bearing down on its second attack even before we can react to the initial bypass: *"Holy Christ!"* In unison—instinctively—we both gesture obscenely as the wailing monster zooms by closer than before. The truck shimmies violently.

Cursing, I dive for the camera pack, yank open the zipper, fumble for the .22. "Here it comes again!" Cassandra yells, flinging herself under the covers. But I've had it, I'm pissed off, and I'm an American protected by a constitution (and the NRA) which entitles me to bear arms, and I'll be damned if I'll sit still for any more of this bullshit.

Thus our placid mesa now bears witness to the confrontation between a naked little fellow (with a hard on and a .22 pistol) and several tons of screaming airborn metal (toting all the latest accouterments of destruction) traveling faster than the speed of sound. I pull back the hammer and take aim, but by the time I fire the plane is already fifty yards beyond my bullet . . . and it keeps blazing north after searing us once more in the retroblast of its hellaciously noisy engines.

Stupified, I watch it recede and disappear; seconds later, only the memory of its passing remains to rattle our composure. With hardly a ruffle, serenity resettles over the mesa.

Cassandra tunnels out from under the bedclothes. "My God," she groans. "Did you hit it?"

"Hell no," I reply scornfully, blowing smoke from the muzzle. "I was only trying to scare him!"

TWENTY

On the mesa I collect nighthawk feathers, aerie bones, prairie dog and coyote skulls, Tres Orejas eagle feathers, a snakeskin from the Sheep Corral Overlook, the jawbones of pocket gophers and pocket mice, white-tipped sage thrasher tail feathers, owl pellets that include mouse skulls imbedded in their tightly-packed fur, the iridescent breast feathers of waterfowl, and the hollow bodies of dung beetles and June bugs. Also a jackrabbit skull, a few small lichen stones, a graceful hunk of sheep vertebrae, and many sprigs of sage.

I take all these gimcracks home and keep them in a box. They are my big medicine bundle. When I travel, bits and pieces of the bundle travel with me. On airplanes, across continents, in strange hotels, I always carry the talismans of life on the quiet mesa.

In Paris I stay at the Hotel de Senlis, on the rue Malebranche, just off the rue St. Jacques, near the Sorbonne and the Parthenon. I'm working on that movie about nuclear war. Upon arriving at the hotel I arrange the contents of my medicine bundle on a table: nighthawk feather, coyote skull, three small bones, a twist of sage. Then I leave to spend the day in a story conference.

After work I stroll along the rue St. Jacques, buying dinner. From the cheese shop I purchase a thick chunk of gruyère. From the bread shop I get half a bagette. The wine shop yields a small bottle of cheap red wine. My favorite deli sells me white cartons of museau, Nice salad, and pickled beets. A news vendor hands over copies of *Le Monde, Figaro, Libération,* and *Le Canard Enchaîné.* Then I turn off St. Jacques onto Malebranche, push into the small hotel, say "Bonsoir" to the concierge, and climb upstairs to my little retreat.

When I open the door, the room smells strongly of sage. Some lichen stones are piled up in a corner. On the brass railing by the open window is a raven—it blinks nervously. A rattlesnake quickly slides under the bed. The burrowing owl perched on the edge of the tub chatters angrily. And a silky pocket mouse, half hidden in the sink drain, sniffs up at me suspiciously—

When I am at loose ends in faraway places, my medicine bundles trigger unquiet dreams of home. Before dawn settles down across the mesa, all vegetation is made resplendent by a blue hoarfrost. Tired from a night of hunting, a coyote tiptoes through the surreal arctic landscape. Sagebrush multiplies upon itself in unending frozen waves. The coyote's shoulder nicks sparkling powder off stiff branches. To the animal's nostrils stick droplets of frozen blood. Limp plumes on the after-fluff of a lark feather are attached to the matted ruff hair on the hunter's neck. No sound do her feet make pattering over the frozen earth.

Paddling forward as gracefully as a seal, I float above the coyote, following her progress. Sky behind the eastern mountains lights up with an aqua blue glow whose luminous intensity soars brighter every second. Unaware of me, the coyote quickens her pace, wanting to reach shelter before dawn breaks. Suddenly, the crestline silhouette of the Sangre de Cristos breaks into matinal fire; mountaintops are laved in bursting gold.

Instantly, the coyote is gone. I had her in my sights, but that wild mountain light diverted my attention for a second. And though there's no place to hide, when I turn back she has become mystery. Her tracks, aiming straight toward Tres

Orejas, end in midstride—the coyote vanishes.

Sunshine hits a hundred square miles of treeless plain all at once and everywhere, melting frost in the blink of an eye. For but a moment steam rises from every dusty arroyo pore; likewise do the branches of sagebrush smoke with vapor— then it all evaporates.

Five minutes later the mesa is dull, hot, dusty . . . boring and unemotional. Miles of blue sky, acres of sage. Nothing moves. Can't make out any significant details. It's gonna be another scorcher.

New York's Helmsley Palace Hotel is a bastion of conspicuous consumption. Compliments, again, of a film company. Still working on that nuclear war story.

My room costs $185.00 a night, and looks down on St. Patrick's Cathedral. When breakfast arrives each morning, a pale pink rose resides in a float bowl on the tray, next to the *New York Times*. Coffee, orange juice, a croissant, and a small ceramic pot of marmalade cost over thirty dollars. I place the float bowl rose on the windowledge, beside a snakeskin, the down feathers of eagles, and the jawbone of a gopher.

Later, quite a commotion arises when a maid enters my ridiculous lap of luxury and finds a vulture dissecting one of the pillows. What truly upsets management, however, is the kangaroo rat who has excavated over a dozen tunnels underneath the rose-colored carpet. To make matters worse for the maid, she can't even clean the toilet because a large brown tarantula is sleeping on the SEALED FOR YOUR PROTECTION paper band wrapped around the seat.

Terror stalks the mesa . . . a man wielding a shotgun is running amok. Horned larks tumble to earth in dusty puffs; low-flying hawks disintegrate into bundles of wild feathers somersaulting at twenty miles an hour through crackling dead sage branches; ravens dive slowly earthward trailing weightless feathery coal.

Like autumn leaves, feathers from all kinds of migratory birds—geese and teal, sandpipers and phalaropes—scatter in droves across abandoned prairie dog towns. They catch in the clawed branches of saltbush; they drift up against rat and rabbit holes; they twirl on the gleaming surface of the stock pond, and by morning are captured in ice.

Rabbits squeal, somersaulting backwards, splashing their brains across black stones. Lizards evaporate in raw gulps of earth knocked loose by lead pellets. Wounded coyotes, trailing saliva and blood, drag themselves through Russian thistles which scratch out their eyes. In midhop kangaroo rats are yanked off by cyclones of .12 gage lead and cast a hundred yards downwind. Stampeding cattle collide with each other, breaking their legs, and tear open their throats galloping through rusty barbwire. And panicked horses rear up, unleashing terrified whinnies.

Barehandedly, he squashes the crickets, breaks rattlesnake backs with a crunching gunbutt, stamps horned toads under thick bootheels. From eight hundred paces deer fall victim to his telescopic legerdemain.

His mouth tears wings apart, spits out feathers; he bites off the heads of shrikes, and uses the weightless bones of larks to pick excrement from his teeth. Surviving animals peer aghast from their burrows . . . then screech backwards in featherless balls of furry gelatinous gunk—nothing escapes the death-dealer.

His succinct genocide he sees as a mission of mercy. The alternative—bulldozers, macadam, sky cranes and steel lattice towers, not to mention the bankers, realtors, and other moneymen—would annihilate the mesa much more cruelly.

Florida is so humid, I doubt my medicine bundle can function here. It's close to ninety-eight in the shade, with a hundred percent humidity, when yet another film company ensconces me at the Fountainbleau Hotel in Miami Beach. Our project concerns Haitian refugees. My room only costs $130.00 a night. The wall-to-wall carpeting is robin's egg blue. Hotel corridors are chock full of security cops protecting the lavish jewelry of Latin American oligarchs and Gusano (and Colombian) drug dealers.

My window overlooks an enormous swimming pool grotto, large as any New Mexico mountain lake. Poolside bars specialize in piña coladas made from real grated coconuts and dark Jamaican rum. A water slide is fun for the kids. Private beaches and the ocean lie beyond. I take one ten-minute swim, and my $13 Timex watch (hidden in a sneaker) is stolen.

Each day I toddle off to palaver (through an interpreter) with Haitian boat people. These mysterious illegal "aliens" recount tales of bitter woe. No doubt my daily expense account adds up to more cash than such poor folks can earn in a year. The paradoxes and contradictions of Miami are almost too heavy to bear. When I return to the hotel drenched in sweat after listening to a dozen sing-song tales of misery, the stretch-limos and black Mercedes suckling at the Fountainbleau's entrance dugs make my stomach heave.

In my room is a disaster. Three nighthawks have broken their necks against the hermetically-sealed windows. Not much else of note has been spawned by the medicine bundle of jackrabbit skulls, killdeer feathers, and rabbit brush twigs.

Yet on the last day, just before bed, I do notice a crust of yellow lichens creeping from the slats in the air conditioner.

Hallucinations about stock pond skating are back. What a stunning ice-cold day. Joy goads me into a trot, leaving Cassandra behind as I hurry along Coyote Gulch toward the dam. My tied-together skates dangle off the shaft of a hockey stick balanced over one shoulder. Crunchy old snow patches encircle every sage bush. The horned larks release peals of chirpy laughter as they flit ahead, leading me to ecstasy. I make crazy faces. I do a little jig step. I try a mummer's strut that soon degenerates into a floppy-jointed scarecrow dance. Cassandra hollers that I've gone bananas. Skate blades clanking together send chiming noises away over the distant swales. On this frigid winter morning, I wish I could do loop-the-loops and alley-oops; I wish I might skate upsidedown across the bottoms of giddy clouds.

Gingerly—at the frozen pond—I test the ice . . . no problem, thick as a moron's skull. My skates I don in a minute, and strut across the unthawed mud, push off, and gliiiiiiiiiide. Oh my gosh—*here at last!* A sixteen-year ambition finally fulfilled.

Happily, I dazzle my friend with pirouettes and figure eights and backwards graceful looping. Then I jump off in speeding circles, stroking hard, working up a sweat, raising my arms in exaltation—!

I'm in Hollywood, now, and all the Guts and Glamour of Tinseltown are embodied for me in the Marina Pacific Hotel, right on the Venice boardwalk. Our film concerns military coups in Latin America, and innocents who are "disappeared" as a result.

From my window I view the street carnival below. Freaks are gadding about on roller skates. Ghetto blasters blare tunes by the BeeGees and Michael Jackson, also Prince, Tina Turner, James Brown—and the B-52s. Spike-haired weirdos are breakdancing on roller skates. Cops in short pants pedal bikes. Half the bums seem twenty-five or younger; they drink beer, wine, and bourbon from paper bags. Basketball and handball games are going full tilt; both male and female body builders are pumping iron on the beach. Men flaunting muscled physiques saunter along the boardwalk wearing short shorts and sandals. Tanned, languid women sport aluminum pink silk T-shirts, silver Spandex bikini-bottoms, and spike heel slingbacks. Add to the brew much graffiti, many street musicians, and plenty of colorful hustlers hawking everything from solar propeller beanies to cocaine. Palm tree fronds flutter wistfully in sea breezes; the beach is crowded with horny bathers. While eating poisonous hot-dogs, Vietnamese fishermen on the pier stare intently into dirty water. Every minute, behind them, a jet thunders off from Los Angeles International Airport.

My talismans are arranged on the night table: two porous red stones from Coyote Gulch, an owl feather, and of course a small bundle of sage.

During a break, I lunch at a boardwalk cafe. Afterwards, I rent skates and dipsy-doodle between palm trees. Couples are necking on the beach. All of us gawk at the crazy manic breakdancers. Soon, my free time is up. Before returning to the story conference, I stop by the room to wash up.

Nothing but sand and red ants splash from the faucets.

Late at night, burnt out and edgy, I call my Taos friend with the Shakespearean moniker. Her sleepy, gravelly voice sounds sexy. "What's happening with the Committee To Save The Mesa?" I wonder.

"Well, sir, the petitions are going okay. Over two hundred names already. We met with the head of the Forest Service and the BLM, and they seemed quasi-receptive. One congressman scheduled a meeting for next week, where five of us will give him an earful. And the electric company had three flunkies to placate us at the last meeting; it seems they're getting nervous. To boot, six days ago somebody spray-painted EAT THE RICH on the Electric Cafe. Also, we carried out that brilliant plan you suggested."

"What plan?"

"A group went to Death Valley, stole a bunch of Devil's Hole pupfish, and planted them in your stock pond."

I'm too pooped for hearty laughter. "And on the negative side of the ledger?"

"Bill Bones got his beer and wine license, and two days later a car full of drunk teenagers drove right over the edge of the gorge."

"Wow! Anybody hurt?"

"No," she answers, icily sarcastic. "The car just dropped

two hundred feet onto a mess of boulders, and the kids all climbed out laughing."

In the end, my Celluloid Land adventures take me to a posh mountain retreat nestled among the Wasatch Mountains near Provo, Utah. The project involves one of my own novels, *The Milagro Beanfield War.* My medicine bundle consists of a snakeskin, some rattles, two hawk feathers, a coyote rib bone, and the ubiquitous sagebrush.

Between story sessions, I check out the grounds. Forty deer are grazing the fifty-acre lawn. Near the house, fat lunker trout inhabit a small pond. Craggy mountains towering above the retreat are beautiful, but also intimidating and claustrophobic. When I depart, a jet ranger helicopter will land on the lawn and whisk me off at treetop level over the mountains to the Salt Lake City airport.

My medicine bundle is confused. It senses the proximity of sagebrush on flats beyond the mountains. It knows deer are close by. Oddly enough, that huge lawn is more intimidating than the concrete and graffiti of New York. And the upshot is, nothing much unfolds. Leaving the shower, I step on a dung beetle; later, rabbit pellets appear on the bedspread, but no rabbits.

Looks like my medicine bundle has lost its chi. Reckon I better mosey on home, then, and forget about all this movie malarky. Time to steer clear of the "real world" for a spell.

And besides, important battles (not to mention loving arms) await me back in Taos.

TWENTY-ONE

F unny how the best laid plans aft gang (gang aft?) agley. On a warm and rare December day, Cassandra informs me that she is leaving Taos. We are at the Sheep Corral Overlook. The sky is as blue as her eyes. Our jackets are lying on the stone; we're both stripped to the waist, soaking up the bennies.

She's heading for southern Mexico, to work in Central American refugee camps. Her son Robert will live with his father in New York; Jennifer just went to the pound. Gently, Cassandra apologizes; her need, finally, is to work at deeper levels than Taos offers. I say nothing; she knows I am puzzled, hurt, angry. She also understands that I respect her choices.

But we have this final afternoon on the mesa together. Cassandra slips off her dungarees and lies on her back on the jackets, head dangling over the cliff edge. Her throat, bent backwards, I could slit cleanly with erotic loving. Tanned and sweetly brown is her dark body. Her arms are cinnamon-colored; her round belly is ample and summery. The blue-veined skin of her wide breasts is very white; her rich pubic hair glistens. The look in her eyes is momentarily passive, very loving. I can smell sagebrush, and feel the unlimited sky reflected off her body. Drowsy afternoon sunlight shines in her blond hair.

A remote world swoons all around us, nothing stirring. She lies hushed, out of character, totally surrendering. I am afraid to touch her smooth and provocative body—she is too beautiful. And there is no way I can capture, control, or otherwise prolong the moment. I yearn to freeze us like this (as I yearn to freeze the mesa), forever.

Everything shines for a beat, agonizingly impermanent. Then it dissipates, the mood changes, the exact spell vanishes.

And I reach down, lightly touching Cassandra.

A week later, I am out on the mesa praying for inclement weather. I wish the fragile territory would become a winter hellhole, driving its handful of human residents across the gorge to warmer houses, closing down its raggedy roads, flinging Bill Bones back to wherever he came from. Let the mesa remind the road builders, realtors, and Reddy Kilowatts eager to exploit it that on earth no more hostile environment exists.

"Be careful what you wish for," friends are always advising me. "You might get it."

Well, at three o'clock on this sunny afternoon the blue sky seems tranquil enough. Yet the moment I step outside the Dodge I am almost sheared in half by the icy wind.

No matter. I'm frustrated, and the violence suits my mood. How else can the mesa defend itself? I flip up my hood, don a woolen cap over that, adjust gloves, strap on the camera pack, grab my tripod, and take off.

Leaning into the wind, I grimace. The temperature may be low twenties, but wind chill factors knock it well under zero. Hard to breathe in the cyclone. Turbulent oxygen whizzes past so rapidly I have trouble sucking it into my lungs. I am caught in invisible shudders, earthquakes of air. Occasionally, cross currents collide violently and things boil up or stop abruptly as two invisible twisters impact—maybe the air stalls . . . but then they squirt around each other, or join ranks, and are off and blasting again.

When I turn my back to the tempest I almost catapult into the White Rock Jumble. So I face the wind again, teeth gritted, eyes almost closed, chest heaving . . . and I curse the weather with fierce, adoring expletives.

I love it when my cheeks go numb, my nose wails, my body shivers. And I want to shout, "Look on *this*, all you mighty developers, and despair!"

I keep my eyes on the ground, otherwise they'll go hopelessly blurry. Roaring fills my head. Despite the cap and hood, my ears are soon too cold—they *ache*. Shifting the tripod from one hand to the other, I place my gloved palm over first this ear, then that one.

Come on, I shout mutely. *Get more hostile. Drive everybody away!*

Indulging in my favorite pastime, I walk up the Western Gully. Pantlegs flap out behind me, straining to be torn off. My frozen patellas begin to sting. But I persist; I *like* the pain. The winged Skull Rock grins mockingly. I duck to avoid a tumbleweed.

As a child, I loved to be tumbled in ocean breakers. I went limp, allowing myself to be buffeted, cuffed, and slammed head-over-heels wherever the wild ocean surges sent me. Walking into the mesa wind reminds me a little of that wacky vitality . . . and insanity.

Suddenly, the wind changes, the sky erupts, warm gusts of air fling big wet snowflakes against me. But wait—the light is exquisite. And, hunched over, I scurry about setting up camera equipment: an aesthetic payoff is imminent.

Rocks are soft and serene; their colors reminiscent of the sepia tinting in old-fashioned photographs. Yet it's nearly impossible to take a picture. Wind splashes snowflakes against the camera lens. My raw, cramped fingers contract. Tripod legs skid off wet rocks. So I give up and race back to the stock pond, where a more golden light filtering through the storm makes me catch my breath. And I *have* to capture this.

Fat chance. Contorting myself, I try to protect the camera and lenses. I wipe the equipment clean every few seconds, racing against the dying light. I shove my fingers into my groin for warmth. The mud is terrible; after five steps my sneakers are ten pounds heavier. I clomp buffoonishly like a circus clown. Twice I skid, taking pratfalls, plunging my fingers deep into freezing goo: it takes minutes of frantic labor to scrape them clean enough to handle the Nikon again. Snot spews from my bulbous red nose.

Nevertheless (I reason), with persistence the photograph will be worth it. Deeper into the adobe glop sink my tripod legs; too bad that I'm ruining them. The picture has become an obsession. Each time I readjust the tripod, my hands come away mud-caked again. Water bubbles off the camera, so I unscrew it, stash it in the folds of my jacket, wipe it dry once more.

A mist rolls up to the stock pond, then mysteriously dissipates. Huge flakes hammer against me for a moment, then subside. Maybe it'll clear up (dream on, MacDuff!). Wind is erratic, playful; it stops, starts, shifts directions five times in three minutes, then unleashes a bevy of staggered blasts. The blurry sky frowns darkly, then lightens up. Visibility of but a hundred yards is replaced by a ten-mile vista. The burnished glow of a setting sun is briefly revealed, then the storm muffles it over, the world turns gray.

My fingers ache, my cheeks sting, my wet feet are *cold*.

For ten minutes the snowy landscape is defined by a passionate ivory-yellow light. Then the horizon slams shut, clouds close over everything, snow begins to fall again. An eerie ferruginous tone embellishes the landscape. Twice I halt, trying to groove on it, but immediately pay for the luxury. Snow zooms directly at me out of the yellow sky. Flakes appear black, like pebbles, and splat against my face.

"Hey, mesa, not me, everybody else—remember? I'm on *your* side."

If I take a photograph, I'm sure the landscape will seem composed and serene.

Ogle it, schmogle it—frostbite threatens. Awkwardly, I trot over the slippery ground, my heavy camera pack jouncing. And with great relief I barge into the truck, cursing the unrepentant elements.

Safe in the protective cab I sit, calming down, watching snowflakes splat against the windshield. Time to go home, but

I cannot move. In a little while I'll turn the ignition key. But right now I just feel like crying.

Bang!

I nearly vault through the ceiling, and, in the same reflexive motion, flop over sideways onto the seat, looking back in terror at the window expecting a killer rock, driven by the wind, to shatter through the glass, pass over my head, and blast out through the passenger window . . . but instead—oh my lurching heart!—there's an agonized bespectacled face and a hairy fist at the window.

I. J. Haynes!

I gulp and straighten up, bug-eyed.

The man looks none too comfortable. His hat is missing, his face is purple, his teeth are chattering; he's wearing a turquoise-silver bolo tie and one of those tweedy western-cut sport coats with leather lapels. The fist made the bang. His blue lips are flapping, and the words—though muffled—I can hear.

"Hey amigo, I need help! Open up!"

"You scared the shit out of me, mister."

"I can't help it. C'mon, open this dang door, lemme in!"

Reaching over, I lift the button, punch open the door, and, accompanied by half the blizzard, I. J. Haynes topples behind the wheel, door slamming shut on his coattails.

"Holy thundering Jesus!" he exclaims. "Am I right glad to see *you*."

"What's the problem?" It's all I can do to control my hostility.

"Oh shoot, you know. I'm sideways in that ditch about a half-mile back yonder. Swerved to miss a goddam coyote. What the hell is a coyote doing out on a day like this?"

"It was thoughtful of you to swerve." My words seem to burble, as if rising from underwater.

"Thoughtful, my ass. I just washed the car. If I get varmint blood all over the grill, Evelyn'll turn eight shades of crimson and kick my butt. Lordy, I'm beginning to hate this stupid mesa."

"I can't help you, Mr. Haynes."

Ever the country buffoon, he grins jovially. "Hey amigo, don't kid around. I'm cold and I'm stuck out in the middle of nowhere. "

"I'm serious. I really can't help you out."

I hear my voice being very calm. Inside, I actually *feel* calm . . . and murderous, capable of terrible things I have never even dreamt of doing before.

"What do you mean, you cain't help?" His voice remains all jocular. "You helped me before, pal."

"That was before. This is now. So if you'd kindly step out of my truck, I'll get on with what I was doing."

The friendliness finally drops off his face with a clunk.

"What were you doing that was so dang important you cain't help a fellow human being in distress?"

"I was having a little nervous breakdown, and I really wanted to have it in private."

While talking, I unzip the camera pack and reach in for my .22 pistol.

"What do you want, money? Okay—" A bank roll emerges from his front trousers pocket. "Here. Here's twenty bucks. Will that make it worth your while?"

The gun is out. Not in my wildest nightmares would I ever actually point a weapon at another person. This one I kind of hold crosswise in my hands, proffering it toward him as I might display a just-caught trout.

"Look, Mr. Haynes. I'm really in no mood to mess with you or your automobile. I'm sorry."

Turns out—thank goodness!—that just the sight of a .22 is enough.

"Hey, pal, whoa—don't get your dander up, I'm leaving, put that thing away—"

Slam!

And he's back in the blizzard, clutching his turned-up lapels closed at the throat, retreating from yours truly, Johnny

the Kid, who just sits there semi-stupified, thinking:
I must remember never to put this gun in my camera pack again.

TWENTY-TWO

D awn brings another shift in the weather's personality; a sloppy rain is falling. The temperature rises to springtime levels; mesa roads must surely be quagmires.

For two days there's no let up; Christmas is upon us. Rain slows to a drizzle; the holiday comes and goes. The world is dreary, soggy, demoralizing—good working weather. Over on the mesa, the Electric Cafe billboard burns to the ground. Within twenty-four hours a new one rises in its place. Quoted in the *Taos News*, Bill Bones has this to say about all that: "You don't get anywhere in life by being a Caspar Milquetoast." Eight readers query the *Taos News* next week: "Casper *who?*"

But given the weather, there'll be no more talk of paved roads or transmission lines until the mesa dries out next spring. And so we are granted a reprieve.

On New Year's, the temperature plummets to nine below zero. It barely rises to fifteen the following day. Next night, same story—but with more wind; I'll bet the chill factor is minus thirty. At dawn, all my windows are made opaque by ice feathers stuck against the panes.

When, on day three, the cold doesn't break, I get a feeling. Like: how much new water entered the stock pond during that rainy time? Access on frozen roads to check it out should be easy—

And faster than anyone ever did it at Le Mans, I sprint for my vehicle.

Ai, what a perfect day! Not a single cloud above. I climb over the fence and proceed along the ridge of Coyote Gulch toward the dam. Rain a few days earlier smoothed the snow crust, then it froze—now all is shiny and sensual. A hullabaloo of lark tracks is visible on the snow, raising a silent ruckus around the Russian thistles. Other tracks reveal that a rabbit fled up the gulch, chased by a coyote.

Careful not to disrupt snow capping the stones, I slip through the White Rock Jumble. Stopping just behind the south edge of the dam, I savor the suspense, then swing around the obstruction—

Well haleluiah.

Enough rain fell to half-fill the stock pond!

And it's frozen over. All the way. And the ice looks clear, dark, and thick enough to hold a person.

I approach the pond. First steps onto a questionable surface are always prudent. The rough shoreline ice holds firm. When I proceed further, however, the ice cracks loudly, sending sharp fracture marks in several directions. I hesitate, calculating my chances, trying to recall where the water is likely to be deep. The north shoreline ice is clear of snow plumes, but looks weakest.

Timidly, I probe further. Most emphatically, I do not wish to fall in. Despite the sun, I figure hypothermia would nail me in a minute if I couldn't escape immediately.

With each step, the ice crackles, shooting out rays of weakness. Yet it seems thick enough: four, five inches. Though "what is thick enough?" I ask myself. Last time I skated on a natural surface was, when?—thirty years ago.

Still, I've waited a long time, and nothing (particularly not my own fear) is going to rob me of the consummation of this day. So, with penguin-small shuffling footsteps, I inch around the skating rink, testing every bit of ice.

Whenever it trembles from my weight, then barks as lightning-shaped cracks zing away from my feet, I freeze. If only clouds would come, blotting out the sun. I wish the day could end now, without further damage. A frigid night would add another few inches to the ice . . . wouldn't it?

By the time I've reconnoitered the entire pond, I'm

convinced the ice will support me. At least if I walk softly, and don't fall down. Whether it'll stand up under the pounding of skate blades is another question. But this matter need not concern us now, because—and here's one for the psychologists—I forgot to bring my skates!

Figure that one out.

For sixteen years I have awaited this opportunity. My Nikon is loaded and rarin' to immortalize the moment. The sun-filled day is perfect. This evening a Chinook might spring up, bringing a sudden thaw . . . or a blizzard. Another morning of Miami Beach rays could sabotage the ice.

But right now, right here, I could do it. I could skate on the stock pond, fullfilling a decades-old dream—

If only I had my blades.

Noon: day two—the prodigal returns.

With renewed vigor (and a pair of skates, a snow shovel, and a hockey stick) I hop into the old Dodge for yet another bright, cloudless outing. Forty minutes later, there I am, on the dam overlooking the stock pond, which just sits there in unblemished glory. For ninety-three million miles not a single microscopic flake anywhere obstructs the sun's rays. It's one of those bland midwinter thawing days over which most people rejoice. I grow apprehensive quickly when the pond, on seeing me, unleashes a tooth-rattling *twang!* that is as loud as a .270 rifle report.

A hint, I gather, that my time may be limited.

Quickly, I lace up the skates. The ice continues to make unhealthy splitting sounds. Urgently, I search for a cloud that might retard the melting process; not within a hundred miles is one in sight. I can actually feel an invisible zone of weather a thousand miles wide shifting gears above North America. A warm pressure front is sliding along a cold rift, flooding southwestern air with heat.

Well, I have been granted a second chance, and do not intend to blow it. Skates tightly tied, I traipse across the still-frozen mud, scamper clumsily over the rough hump ice near shore, then stroke onto a smoother surface.

Such groans of protest! New fracture veins chatter off at every step I take. The ice cracks and echoes; I squeak, flinch, and squeal, testing the ice not so much with my body as with my heart. I carry the hockey stick crosswise; perhaps it'll save me from falling completely through a hole. . . .

But I don't get off the ice; I intend to push this experience to the limit. I circle once, four, seven times. Though it continues to complain, the ice holds. Obviously, I am charmed and nothing can go wrong. Otherwise, why did the stock pond freeze in the first place?

Soon I am fearless and cocksure. Round and round I skate, first clockwise, then counterclockwise; then I cut all sorts of fancy figures, feeling wacky and intoxicated.

Never does the ice cease kvetching, yet despite the noise, it holds me. And so I lean into it, zooming, or I simply coast along, happiness flipped round my neck like a scarf, its merry tassels fluttering behind me as I bask in an awareness of the near sagebrush mesa, the distant Tres Orejas, and the immaculate space between.

Often in the past I wondered how this experience would be. Paraphrased words of Gertrude Stein often came to mind: "What if, when we get There, we find that there is no There there?" Yet today, philosophical reflections seem irrelevant. If it feels good, graceful, fully alive, what other point is there?

A small plane, that departed Taos airport a minute ago, flies overhead, droning west. Were I up there gazing down at a single person skating on a small isolated stock pond, I know I'd smile, and carry the image with me for awhile.

On winter days the sun moves fast. Frozen mud around the pond is thawing. If I want a picture from the top of the dam, I better hustle. Awkwardly, I trudge toward the crest, lugging my equipment. In the old days I would have screamed at anyone who so abused a pair of skates! Today, I barely grimace as my hollow-ground blades crunch against pebbles, sticks, and bigger stones. It ain't easy to maintain balance on the steep slope.

Once tripod and camera are set up, I must choose a path of least resistance back to the ice. It's a task for a Hollywood stunt person. I plan each step over boulders, through rabbit brush, down the final patch of mud onto the ice. Then I set the timing lever, punch the button, and take off, with eight seconds to D-Day!

Headlong crazy, counting aloud, I dive toward the pond. My ankles bend at each clumping step, but they don't snap. I teeter, wildly pinwheeling my arms for balance, cantering fast as possible down through the garbage, skidding as I hit the half-frozen mud, and, first time onto the pond my feet sail out from under and I take a sensational header onto the ice, which—thanks God!—doesn't break.

Blades sinking into adobe glop, I trudge back up the hill, reset the camera, punch the button, and fly south again. The technique, I soon learn, is to fling aside all caution, be damned if I bust a leg or shatter a skate blade, and just hump it helter-skelter down the rocky hill, so that by the time I hit the muddy part of the obstacle course I'm almost striding at full speed onto the ice.

A dozen times I execute this bizarre and dangerous manuever. The process leaves me sucking on my asthma inhaler—and hooting insanely between blasts!

Then, stretched out on my back, I gaze at the sky. Never has it seemed so blue. Beneath me, the ice cracks softly, shooting out more veins of weakness. Now would be a fine time for disaster to strike, while I'm limply cradled in sunshine, dazzled by blueness: the ice parts, frigid water swallows me whole, the shock stops my heart—*bingo!*—and six months hence a hardhat erecting a steel tower discovers my bones at the bottom of a dry hole, surrounded by tiny clam shells.

Instead, I simply lie there, calming down. An entire sky without a cloud enters an entire brain without a thought. I am hypnotized, weakened by happiness: I chuckle. And when I rise, aching pleasantly all over, I skate some more, tasting it until I've had my fill.

The sun leans toward the west, the white full moon ascends into the regal blue sky. Only then do I scuffle off ice into soft mud, advance onto harder ground, shuck off the skates and call it a day.

At eleven that night I find myself thinking about the frozen stock pond. The fantasy makes me shiver, yet the mesa has its siren call, and it's too beautiful a night—I finally decide—to waste. So for the second time today I drive over to the stock pond.

During daylight hours the mesa is an empty place. At night it is hauntingly deserted. Again, there's no wind. The full moon grows brighter by the minute. While I'm tightening skate laces, the ice cracks with heart-rending echoes that sound ten times nastier than they did at two P.M.

When all is set, I hesitate. Clearly, this is an enchanted night. Moonlight makes the sky almost blue. About the only constellation visible is the Big Dipper. For 360 degrees the horizon is lit up, as if a single circular city were casting a haze of luminosity into the atmosphere.

The night seems extraordinarily buoyant. A ring of snow surrounds the stock pond. Mud is frozen solid. The eastern mountains stand out clearly; an ivory mist of illumination expands up off their peaks and ridges.

Such an iridescent nocturnal transparency—landscape bathed in a chiffon light, air sparkling with taffeta mystery.

During the day the mesa cannot expand beyond that ninety-three million miles to the sun. But at midnight it extends to the farthest star in our galaxy, and whatever else is visible beyond. The darkness doesn't enclose, it expands.

Well, the ice beckons and so I glide onto the pond and coast around slowly. Earlier, the TV news explained that tomorrow will be another scorcher—so this ice is doomed. Already, it seems to be weakening toward a fail-safe point. The spooky renting noises are more frequent, and louder; obviously, my minutes are numbered.

Yet on I skate, floating around in a dark blur, cold air whistling past my ears. After a while I throttle back and tiredly drift. I perspire warmly, and the reflected moon slides beside my feet. Noodling along lackadaisically, I savor what is left to me of this night; sadly, I admit the adventure is almost over. The mesa hums in silence. Plans for its development filter into my awareness, I push them out. The surrounding world is covered by bright crystals, and I myself am coolly alive and sensuous, silvered by the night: I cast a long dark shadow across the frosted world.

My arms, my eyes, my heart I extend into all this space. And I remember the night I lay in the truck with Cassandra, feeling intensely connected to everything . . . and the sensation excites me again as memories of the mesa rise through the cold.

The small rattler, the trigger-happy duck hunters, yellow swallowtails and horned larks, the stalled Edsel, bragging Bill Bones, good ol' I. J. Haynes, and loving Cassandra. The faces—at our meetings—of those decent souls concerned about the future of this fragile plateau arrange themselves in the air around me. I wish I could share with all of them this winter ecstasy.

Phalaropes, the pteradactyl ibis, the Winged Skull Rock, bald eagles and sparrow hawks and ravens, bones and nighthawks and the lichen rock, spadefoot tadpoles . . . and even Jennifer. It all rises in me with a bittersweet rush. I think of Cassandra in the refugee camps; I see eighty-six-year-old Andres Martínez talking to the sheep and cattle ranchers; I recall the gray-haired lady asking me for a reason to be hopeful. I hear an old man after the Los Cordovas meeting talking about the weather . . . and I fervently hope that when *I* die they will fill up my grave with sunshine.

And for whatever reasons, for *all* the reasons, I am encouraged by the future, and not afraid of the slaughter-house. Balanced again, cured by the mesa, ready for anything.

I am forty-four, but feel young: and no matter what struggles are in store, my heart will always have this wild place to be in.

It occurs to me, then, that in this rich midnight solitude I could be a child upon the moon. And impulsively I let go, losing all my fears—I leave my feet and it is just as the astronauts said it would be. Down I go in slow motion, laughing because I know I won't be hurt. Twisting in mid-air, I roll my face to the stars . . . and cast a goofy wink at the moon. And when I land against the ice, it breaks, slivers and chips and bright shards erupting without a sound all around me—yet even then I am unconcerned and unafraid. Pieces of glittering crystal fan out above me as I sink beneath the ice, my hands unabruptly reaching for the sky, my feet paddling nonchalantly through the weird muffling explosion . . . and there is no cold water to kill me, none at all. Instead, only dry dusty air occupies the stock pond bowl under its frozen lid, and through that air—perhaps twelve feet deep—I fall, landing harmlessly on my back among phosphorescent clam shells and bleached old coyote bones, and puffs of yellow pollen that billow around my body in wonderful unfurlings of lightness.

Lying still, I gaze stupidly back up at the jagged aperature through which I tumbled. Pieces of ice settle quietly around me. The frozen covering above is crisscrossed by blade slashes which catch moonlight as if in a shimmering web. The hole I made is many-pointed, like a star. Things drifting through the air under here include dry juajolote skeletons and shriveled spadefoot bodies, some killdeer feathers, and tufts of rabbit fluff.

At peace, posed with arms and legs outstretched among the bones as if to make a dust angel, I catch the shadow of footsteps crossing above me. Knees touch the ice near my hole; dark palms press down right at the opening; a face appears—Cassandra.

"Hey you down there!" She laughs. "I brought you something."

And off her fingertips twirls a papery gift. It zig-zags like a leaf toward me, taking plenty of time.

"Just another poem," she calls. "To help keep the faith, reinforce connections, stay powerful."

I catch it, focus my eyes, and struggle to make out the words. It was penned—not so long ago—by an anonymous El Salvadoran:

> . . . I believe that the world is beautiful,
> and that poetry is like bread, everyone's.
>
> And that my veins do not end inside me,
> rather in the unanimous blood
> of all those who struggle for life,
> love,
> things,
> countryside and bread,
> the poetry of all.

"That's it?"

"No, there's one more thing." Her hand stretches out, silhouetted against the night heavens. She lets go of something terribly insignificant. It begins as a tiny white fleck at her fingertips, and descends dreamily, end-over-end until it grows almost to the size of a snowflake. I reach up and catch it in the bowl of both hands cupped together: a bone, that tiny perfect trinket we found together at the aerie: weightless, shaped like a paddle, mysteriously powerful in its intrepid smallness.

"A mosquito could row across the galaxy with such a bone!" her voice proclaims, echoing strangely into this hollow pond.

"Are you coming down here with me?" I ask.

"Nope. I'm off to the old rat race, kiddo. The world calls. I got miles to go before I sleep. You hold down this fort, okay?"

"Well . . . sure, okay."

"So long, Mr. Nichols—and don't forget: "'The most powerful weapon people have against a common enemy is optimism.'"

185

"I won't forget."

She puts out a fist against the sky; I raise my own fist in return; and in unison, we salute each other.

"Hasta la victoria siempre!"

EPILOGUE

During the night snow has fallen. Duke nudges me awake at
five A.M., eager to go out. For a minute I lie still,
disoriented. I forgot to close the curtains, and a surreal light
infuses the room, as if a million distant candles were casting a
gleam across the valley. When I climb out of bed and shiver
through the freezing house to the kitchen door, I discover it's
only from the storm.

Duke marches out the front door and stops on the portal
stoop, surprised by the snow. Almost eight inches cover the
ground. A fairy-tale Christmas hush holds the world. Duke
can't deal, so he trots back inside. I tarry, enjoying the noise-
proof valley. Rarely am I awake at this secret hour.

The cat follows me back to bed and curls up on the
sleeping bag. But I cannot drift off right away, phantom light in
the bedroom is too special. It makes me tingle a bit.

Though I know sunshine will butcher me awake too early,
I won't close the curtain. And, bathed in soft light, Duke purring at my feet, I fall asleep.

Same day, a few hours later, I'm cursing the ultrabright
sunshine glaring off my pillow. Yet on such a white morning,
who can grumble for long? I stoke up the wood stove, light a
fire under the coffee water, feed Duke and let him out, then
realize: hey, it's cold! Down into fat moonboots I jam my blue
toes. More small logs have to come in from the woodbin. Then
I don my jacket, dip up a mayonnaise jar of birdseed from a

garbage can on the portal, and circle the house to clear the feeders and scatter the hen scratch. Two dozen grackles and some starlings are already waiting in the locust trees.

Morning rituals call for a glass of orange juice, vitamin pills, and coffee, while I clip and file yesterday's paper. Then I bundle up and walk to the outhouse. There I linger with the door open, enjoying the woodpile heaped with snow, the four tall aspens I planted sixteen years ago, the garbage cans sporting eight-inch-high snow caps, and the apple and pear trees behind the garden. A chicken wire fence around the abandoned animal pens has a latticework of undisturbed snow. Fence posts wear eight-inch cone hats. Beyond the back field, a woodsmoke haze lies over town. Through it I can barely make out a silhouette of the Cañon Hills. Dimmed by the pollution, two horses in a field seem like ghosts.

Clearly, this day was not meant to be wasted in mundane workaday pursuits. Just like that, I blow off my obligations, hop in the truck, and head west. Beyond the gorge, I park on the highway and walk south onto the mesa.

A lone 4-wheel drive has assayed the main road. I follow the ruts for half a mile, then strike out across the glaring wasteland. Everything is buried. Sage bushes and snakeweed clumps resemble igloos. Taller rabbitbrush branches are splayed and bent by heavy snow overcoats. A few tall grasses stand out, their yellow stalks a welcome contrast to the unending and total whiteness.

Across this moon I wander, pausing to take photographs. At intervals I halt, responding to the environment by staying quiet, by listening to the silence, by letting myself relax. For miles no tracks tell stories in the unblemished mantle. Have all the small hibernators been suffocated already? I expected fresh holes where rabbits and kangaroo rats had tunneled out. Yet all I come across, finally, is a single raven-sized wing print in the powder.

All snowdunes slant gracefully in a northeasterly direction. The wind must have whistled last night. I'm glad it's shut down now. My eyes soon hurt from squinting.

I pass black and brown cows mournfully standing around, wondering: what next? Steam boils out of their nostrils. Mountains are bleached from top to bottom, and their whiteness merges with the snowy mesa, and the snowcover travels west until it fades into the cerulean blue atmosphere.

Near the stock pond I climb the fence. Details of Coyote Gulch are lost under snow. All along the north rim of the gulch are the hieroglyphic scribbles of lark feet—at last, a sign of life! The birds have been feasting on Russian thistles. Though all else may be dormant, the horned larks are always around, busy and chipper, joyously hardy. They are the first wild breed to sound an all clear and get right back to business.

While I read their stories, the larks surround me, tame as you please, pecking thistle seeds. For a long time I study their petite orthographies among the nearly-submerged thistles: such *busy* markings.

Then I climb onto the dam. The nearly-evaporated stock pond is covered by a mushy yellow crust. It sits in an unblemished disc of whiteness. No tracks lead to the ice. Though only three P.M., the day has become cold; sunlight grows thin. Clouds have risen from both horizons. I take pictures. Suddenly, I'm surrounded by small wings as two hundred finches land all around me. They splash about in the dry nettles, twittering excitedly. Then I move an arm too rapidly, and they all jump up and zip away.

Gray clouds lift higher in the east, shrouding the mountains. Above the clouds that intense blue sky remains. The horned larks fly away, leaving the area completely silenced. Shadow swoops over the stock pond and dam, and sluices eastward to the base of the mountains. For ten minutes a thin streak of sunshine travels along the foothills under the clouds.

Not bad, not bad at all. Tres Orejas stands out cleanly in the numinous silence. Between the harsh drouth of summer and this bewitching winter hour lie a thousand small adventures that have endeared the mesa to my heart, and also defined its mortality.

It may be a land of marginal life . . . yet for me it has been a world of dazzling affirmation. Certainly it is a place worth fighting for.

When I start back, I follow the tire ruts on the road. Obviously, no other truck will come along; I have the road and the mesa to myself. Twilight cold has made the dry snow sound rusty. Slowly, I squeak north.

The colder the mesa, the warmer and more wonderfully isolated I feel. Immaculate snow extends everywhere. All life is submerged beneath the white darkness. Only I am in motion; larks are roosting; no coyotes will travel tonight. Great horned owls await better weather for hunting. Animals sleep for their lives as I tramp through the iceberg stillness.

Glittering frostflowers make gems of roadside rabbit brush. While the mesa hangs in serene killer limbo, I proceed toward home impervious to frostbite. Nanook of Taos k-flops along, toting a tripod instead of a harpoon, nibbling on a Mars Bar instead of whale blubber.

On purpose I slow down. I don't want to leave the beguiling frozen plain. This evening ends a cycle, it finishes a year-long rhythm of life. Seldom before has this land and its denizens come to such a complete standstill. Tomorrow, I'm sure, a process will commence anew. Things will dig out, make tracks, start hunting. Owls will ruffle their feathers and blink, waking up hungry. And Bill Bones will go to work, fire up the grease bins, dump in some french fries.

But right now this arctic mood belongs solely to me. I own the mountains; the sky begins expanding an inch above my shoulders. The solitude creates a rapture inside me. Pale salmon clouds stretch along the north horizon. Angus cows are pressed together in a clump of rabbit brush, their breath a halo above them.

Creak, creak, my boots advance. Until, for the last time, I halt, turning a circle, gazing all around. I don't want to lose it, I suppress feelings of loss. Perhaps I can't ever reproduce the satisfaction of this moment; maybe I'll never again have such reverence for life. It doesn't matter. The most precious gifts often dissolve off my fingertips within a moment of their triumphs: a nude woman at the edge of a cliff, four avocets feeding, a midnight skate on the stock pond.

We are touched by magic wands. For just a fraction of our day life is perfect, and we are absolutely happy and in harmony with the earth. The feeling passes much too quickly. But the memory—and the anticipation of other miracles—sustains us in the battle indefinitely.